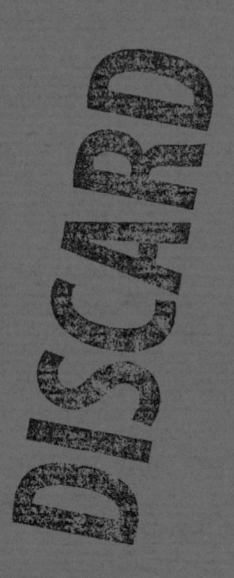

Sagebrush Seed

Sagebrush Seed

Don Ian Smith

ABINGDON   NASHVILLE

SAGEBRUSH SEED

Copyright © 1977 by Abingdon

Library of Congress Cataloging in Publication Data

SMITH, DON IAN. 1918–
   Sagebrush seed.
   1.   Nature   (Theology)—Meditations.   I.   Title.
BT695.5.S64   242'.4   77-4347

ISBN 0-687-36746-8

Scripture quotations unless otherwise noted are from the Revised Standard Version Common Bible, copyright © 1973. Scripture noted Phillips is from The New Testament in Modern English, copyright © J. B. Phillips 1958, 1960, 1972.

MANUFACTURED BY THE PARTHENON PRESS AT NASHVILLE, TENNESSEE, UNITED STATES OF AMERICA

Dedication

To my children, Heather, Rockwell, and
Heidi, whose ability to enjoy and
appreciate the good things of life has
added so much to the life that Betty and I
enjoy and share together.

Acknowledgments

When one writes from his own experience, and uses very few direct quotations, there is a tendency to forget the great contribution made by those with whom he lives and works—those who give perhaps the greatest contribution of all, inspiration. Since most of this book has been developed in one form or another in the sermons preached at Hillview United Methodist Church, Boise, Idaho, over the past few years, I would be less than honest if I did not acknowledge that the affection, patience, and loyal support of the people of Hillview gives me the strength and inspiration to try to bring to their pulpit, week by week, the best witness that I can. Without the joy of sharing my faith with this congregation of sincere Christians, who in charity consistently encourage my best, and overlook my worst, I could not preach, and I probably would not write.

I am especially grateful to our church secretary, Mrs. Gordon Snell, who has graciously stretched her job description to include all of the typing needed to edit, correct, and prepare this manuscript.

Preface

I was born and raised on a farm—a country boy. As far as has been possible for one who was called to the profession of the ministry, I have remained a country man. Though I presently serve a suburban congregation, the first twenty-eight years of my ministry were in rural areas, and I am still able, by living on an acreage a few miles from the church, to keep my favorite hobby of working with the land, the changing seasons, and my favorite animals—horses. During a long pastorate at Salmon, Idaho, I and my family owned, operated, and lived on Sky Range Ranch in the very heart of central Idaho's majestic mountains. Sky Range Ranch is now the home of our daughter, Heather, her husband, Lynn Thomas, and their two children, Michael and Andrea.

The out-of-doors has always stimulated in me a sense of awe and a mood of worship. As I share with my reader my love of nature, I do not want in any way to imply a worship of nature. I lift my eyes to the hills, but I know my strength does not come from the hills. It comes from the God who made the hills, who is our dwelling place in all generations and was even ''before the mountains were brought forth or ever thou hadst formed the earth and the world.'' (Ps. 90:2). As Christians we worship the creator, not the creation. Trying to see God only through the world of nature, we see neither God nor nature very clearly. But what a wonderful world of nature there is to see and enjoy when it is seen through the eyes of faith, seen in the light of God's love, seen by one who knows that ''he is our God, and we are the people of his pasture'' (Ps. 95:7).

It is my desire to share with my reader ways in which my love for and close relationship with the world of nature has brought me a deeper appreciation of God who best reveals his love for us through Jesus Christ who walked the good earth and liberally illustrated his message with vines and trees, fish and birds, seeds, harvests, sheep and shepherds.

God's ways are not always our ways, and in choosing the title *Sagebrush Seed* I want to share something of the sense of awe and wonder that Isaiah must have felt when he spoke of God's bringing forth a tender plant out of dry ground (Isa. 53:2). From our limited human point of view we would look only in moist ground for a tender plant, forgetting that our God is able to bring new life to that which we have considered hopeless, dried up, and dead. From my life-long love affair with nature there has come an increasing faith in him who holds all nature in his hand and ''is able to do far more abundantly than all that we ask or think'' (Eph. 3:20).

Don Ian Smith
Boise, Idaho

Contents

Sagebrush Seed

Quite a few years ago we were involved in building a new church and parsonage in the town of Salmon, Idaho. The old church and parsonage had been built down in the old part of town along the river bottom. The Salmon river flows right through the town and the city park is an island in the river. When we built the new church and parsonage we built in a section of town known locally as The Bar. The Bar is so named because it is in fact a huge bar, like a sand bar, that was formed over a period of thousands of years as the earth in the canyon behind the town washed out onto the river plain. Such bars, often called benches, are very common in the Rocky Mountains—there is nearly always one of some size at the mouth of every canyon. The one at Salmon is two or three miles long and makes an excellent building base for a good part of the residential portion of the small town.

Much of The Bar is formed of gravel and larger rocks, and, in the area where we built, it provides an excellent condition for the foundations of buildings— no problem with mud or earth slides. There is no danger of a building's sinking. The rock and gravel is very firm, but also porous, and there is not enough topsoil to make a good lawn and landscape. So when we built our parsonage, we leveled the rocks and covered them with earth moved in from somewhere else. Because the rocks make such a porous base, it is almost impossible to keep enough water on the ground to grow a good lawn unless you first cover the rocks with a heavy soil like clay that will keep the water from your lawn sprinkler from sinking right down into the ground to river level. We brought in some very heavy clay from an excavation being made for a building down in the river bottom. We covered the rocks with the clay, but found that the clay was not very good for making a seedbed. We then went out into the sagebrush covered foothills not far from town to get some high-quality topsoil—enough to cover the clay to a depth of two or three inches. With this we were able to make an excellent seedbed; we seeded our lawn and with great anticipation turned on the sprinklers. We were not disappointed. We got a fine stand of grass and in a short time had a good lawn. But we also got something we had not expected—a most wonderful crop of beautiful little sagebrush plants. They were no problem to the lawn. One mowing when they were about two inches high would finish them off and leave the grass in good shape to crowd them out. But they were so pretty, and there were so many of them, that before mowing them we did pot a large number and sold quite a few of them to tourists as a way of raising a little more money for our church building program and as a way of advertising a mission project we had under way at the Salmon Church.

Many times in the years since we grew that fine crop of tiny, beautiful sagebrush plants, quite by accident, I have thought of them and realized how symbolic they are of the joy, life, hope, and goodness that can grow in any human life, but which often lies dormant, waiting for the right conditions to cause them to sprout and grow and reach up for the sun.

When we brought in the topsoil from the hillside it was not obvious that it was filled with dormant sagebrush seed. New sagebrush does not sprout on the hillside in profusion every year. Sage is a dry-land plant and can survive a great deal of drought once it is established. The annual precipitation on the low hills around Salmon, Idaho, is about twelve inches per year or less, which means this land is classified as desert. Most of the plants we think of as crops will do well only with irrigation. There are many years when conditions are not right for sagebrush to sprout and get established. But year after year the sagebrush puts forth its seeds to be dropped into dry ground. Most of the sagebrush seed that we brought into our lawn had probably been lying dormant in the dry earth for a number of years, perhaps as many as ten or fifteen. The seed lies in the earth—dry, dormant, apparently dead, but waiting for a special springtime, a certain season when there will be more than average moisture and conditions will be just right. Then, even if it has been dormant for many years, it will come to life, produce a new and lovely plant, just as if it were newly created and had never had to wait through all the dry and disappointing years. And when we brought the sagebrush seed into our new lawn, our sprinkler furnished the right conditions. Moisture and sunshine

13

touched the dried seed; conditions were right for that special springtime; and, from the almost perfect stand of sagebrush that came up, I think that nearly ever seed must have sprouted.

The ability of seeds, roots, and some kinds of bulbs to remain dormant for long dry periods, then suddenly develop new life under the right conditions is one of the most interesting facts of the natural world. It is a wonderful illustration of the hope that lies hidden within us all, the hope of new life in many areas of our personalities in which we may have experienced spiritual dryness for many years. Isaiah, speaking of the power of God to change life and bring power in place of weakness, has something like this in mind when, in the beginning of the fifty-third chapter, he asks with awe: "Who has believed what we have heard? And to whom has the arm of the Lord been revealed? For he grew up before him like a young plant, and like a root out of dry ground. . . ." A root out of dry ground—a new plant from a shriveled seed—what a symbol of the new life the Christian finds through faith when he opens his heart and soul to the love of God. The apostle Paul found it so amazing that he speaks of one becoming a "new creature," a whole new person in that special springtime that comes when one puts aside one's shriveled, dried-up, self-centered life and allows the power of God to do what moisture and sunshine can do for the dormant sagebrush seed.

Sagebrush seed says something to me; I never travel through one of our great sage-covered areas of the West without thinking about it. A creator who can keep the spark of life alive in a seed, in the shallow, dry, hot soil of the desert for years and years if need be, while waiting for that special springtime when the rains come, can certainly bring back to life in me and in other people, qualities of life that we may have considered dead and almost forgotten. Love that we thought had

14

died can blossom again if given the right conditions; the wonder of childhood that made each new day a joy can be restored and once more we can welcome each new sunrise with a prayer of thanksgiving and listen expectantly for the song of birds. Bitterness toward our fellowmen may have developed over years of spiritual dryness, but honestly confessing our own faults, humbly accepting the forgiveness of one who forgave even those who crucified him, and then forgiving others, even as we have been forgiven, can bring that special springtime in our lives, and like a root out of dry ground we find our own lives responding. Shoots of fellowship, joy, and love begin to grow.

I have lived almost all my life in sagebrush country. Sagebrush is not a spectacular plant like a great redwood tree or a flowering dogwood. But it is a wonderful part of creation. It is food and shelter for many creatures. It serves a very vital role in the control of erosion. But most of all, for me, it is living evidence that God never gives up. His ways are often quite different from my ways. What I might call hopeless failure may be for him a time of opportunity; what from my point of view may be death may be for him only a period of dryness, a testing of patience, a period of drought before the rain comes and the desert blooms again.

For many Christians a mustard seed is a symbol of faith, and it is a good one (Luke 13:19), but for me there is no better symbol of the power and mercy of God than the seed of the sage, so like our small and limited human lives that can appear so hopeless and yet have within them the ability to respond with new life when conditions are made right by one who ''stands at the door and knocks,'' only waiting for us to open it; one who promises that he ''will wipe away every tear from their eyes'' and says: ''Behold, I make all things new'' (Rev. 21:4, 5).

Good Grass Grows

Grass is the healer of the earth. Grass is nature's Band-Aid when the earth is injured; it is nature's long-range therapy to mend wounded land and make it well again.

Grass is one of the reasons man cannot destroy the earth. Grass is one of the reasons I am optimistic about the future. Man may destroy himself—he has been doing it individually and in groups since the beginning of creation—but he will not destroy the earth. "The earth is the Lord's," and God has grass on his side. Man can hurt the earth and thereby hurt himself, but the healing grass will continue to grow.

When the surface of the earth is injured by careless men with too many bulldozers or by an act of nature itself, such as forest fire or flood, as soon as the irritant is removed the healing grass begins its work. Tiny blades appear. Tiny rootlets begin to bind the broken earth together. It may take only a season; it can take many years, depending on the extent of the injury. Time is not as important to God as it is to humans. We have only a lifetime; he has eternity.

The grass does come and heal the earth. Like injured skin and flesh, given just a little care and a little help to make conditions right, the healing takes place quite rapidly.

In the 1930s great portions of America became "dust bowls." Bad farming practices and years of drought made lovely farmlands, gardens, and meadows into frightening deserts. In Kansas I have seen sand dunes and stumps of dead trees in a place that had once been a fruit orchard with a pleasant swimming hole for children. With the dead trees stood the dead dreams of a family.

For the nation it was a terribly costly lesson in our need to learn about and cooperate with the forces of nature. People did learn, and the rains returned to the earth and the grass healed the land. The sand dunes were leveled, trees were replanted, and again there are happy children splashing in the old swimming hole.

To me grass is a great symbol of the Creator's desire and ability to heal what is broken, to rest those who are weary, to restore to wholeness that which is damaged. It is no coincidence that the Psalmist found his soul restored beside still waters in "green pastures." In the world of nature, green is the color of health and restoration.

I have had a life-long love for grass. I cannot remember a time without an appreciation of grass. In my earliest childhood memory there is the joy of feeling new grass against my bare feet. Since that time I have made grass into hay for my livestock; I have grazed my cattle on it in summer; and I have slept on it in the mountains. Even now, as I write, I look out my study window and thank God for a soft rain that came last night—a rain that means an acre of bare ground behind our church soon will turn into a great green carpet where the children of our community can play.

We hear and read a good deal these days about land being abused by livestock's overgrazing. It does still occur, but most of the serious abuse of public lands took place prior to 1940; since that time we have made wonderful and steady progress in land management. Grass-eating animals are a necessary and important step in the process of turning grass into much needed food for people. We must not let past mistakes in land management blind us to the fine progress that we have made in managing our grasslands.

The reason an overgrazed grassland often is marked by coarse, undesirable plants is not because the bad plants are so hardy, but because the grass is so good that the horses, cattle, or elk eat the grass and leave the unpalatable plants to reproduce themselves. If we change the grazing season just a little bit to favor the grass, and if we reduce the number of animals to a level consistent with what range managers call a sustained yield, then the good grass grows and in time will take over the ranges. The good grass is a tough competitor. It bears out the truth that good is stronger than evil, and in the long run it always will win.

Some years ago I was one of a group of ranchers who worked with the Bureau of Land Management on a range renewal project. We had several hundred acres of rangeland that once had been good grazing land but had been overgrazed for many years and was producing almost nothing but sagebrush. Our reseeding program involved plowing up the sagebrush, planting a tough, drought-resistant variety of grass which was not native to the area, and fencing the area. It was fenced so that the new exotic grass could have three years to become well established before cattle began grazing on it.

By the end of three years an interesting fact emerged. There were areas that had been too rough for us to plow and seed, and in these areas the native grasses had renewed themselves so well that we questioned the need for having reseeded with the exotic grass.

All over our Western ranges we are finding that to restore rangelands to top production we do not need to replace native grasses and often do not need to remove competing plants—though it sometimes helps to speed up the restoration. We need simply to control grazing so that the good native grasses have a fair chance of competing with the unpalatable plants like sagebrush. Given a fair chance, the native grasses not only will compete but will take over their rightful, dominant place in the ecology of the land. If we have the patience to wait a year or two we will find this same principle working in the making of a good lawn, and, given the right treatment, the high-quality grasses will crowd out undesirable weeds.

The remarkable toughness of the good grasses, which gives them the ability to compete with and replace less desirable plants on a range, has become, for me, a symbol of a fact of creation. Good is stronger than evil, and the Christian faith rightly puts more stress on cultivating that which is good than on trying to stamp out that which is bad. A Christian naturally will oppose what is bad and destructive to the good life for himself and others, but the person who becomes more concerned with "rooting up evil" than he is with appreciation and cultivation of "whatever is true, whatever is honorable, whatever is just, whatever is pure, whatever is lovely, whatever is gracious'' (Phil. 4:8) has misread the gospel.

One of the most interesting of the parables of Jesus speaks directly to this point. A farmer had a good crop of wheat, but an enemy had planted weeds among the grain. Eager servants came to the farmer seeking his order to go into the field and pull up the weeds. But the wise farmer said, ''No; lest in gathering the weeds you root up the wheat along with them'' (Matt. 13:29). The farmer had the wisdom to know that the good wheat was an able competitor and that harvest time was soon enough for the wheat and weeds to be separated. He knew it was far more important to concentrate on giving the good wheat a proper chance to grow than it was to do violence to it and trample it in a misguided emphasis on rooting up the weeds.

There is something in the very nature of creation that is on the side of goodness and truth, and we mortals very quickly can do more harm than good by an overzealous effort to become the judges of others, seeking to purge the earth of evil.

History bears out the tragic story of blood and tears needlessly spilled by the witch hunters, inquisitors, and zealots who have lost sight of the natural power of goodness and have seen their calling to be the eliminators of evil. Every reformer desiring to make truly worthwhile contributions to society would do well to ponder this truth: God is on the side of good, and it is more important to build up than to tear down. The reformer would do well to sit quietly on a mountainside or ride across a great green prairie and give thanks to God for the wonder of good grass that grows—grass that grows even where no man planted it; grass that will flourish and continue to heal the land long after the reformers and those with whom they contended have been laid to rest beneath it.

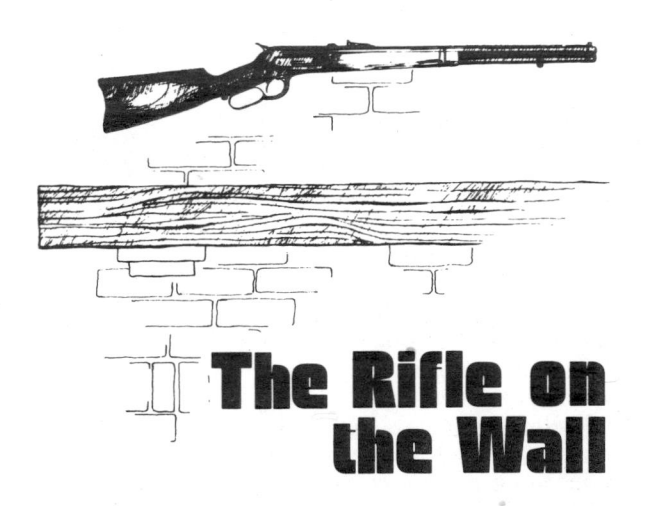

The Rifle on the Wall

When I think about the cabin home of a frontier family I visualize most of the activity around the large fireplace. The fireplace was the only source of heat in the home and often at night it was the principal source of light. So here the family gathered to eat its meals, do its work, and enjoy what recreation they could make for themselves. Over the fireplace hung a rifle. It was the best rifle the family could afford. It hung over the fireplace because that was where the family would likely be when the rifle was needed to protect the home. It was in the center of the families' life in the home, and if they traveled it was taken along and kept close at all times. This was a "working" rifle. It provided protection for the home, meat for the table, and was a great source of comfort and security to the frontiersman when he traveled, his companion on the long lonely watches of the night.

In our home we have a fireplace. Over the fireplace hangs a rifle. It is in good working condition—though at present I have no ammunition for it. It is a 45-70 in a model used in the 1870s and in good condition because it came from the factory in 1884 and was used very little since a better model was soon developed.

I cherish this rifle. It is a fine conversation piece, and among gun fanciers, it can even be the source of a good argument. It is not for sale, because I like having it on the wall above the fireplace. My interest in it is, however, purely sentimental and intellectual. I never use it. It does not provide protection for my home; it does not put meat on our table; it is not my comfort and security in the time of trouble. It really does not make a bit of difference in my way of life.

Every person needs a religious faith that makes a difference in his way of life—a religion that is the first thing he reaches for in the time of trouble, a faith that is near to the center of family life, one that goes with him in the working world and helps put meat on the table. He needs a faith that is a real comfort and companion in the lonely watches of the night. For the "working" faith one needs, one cannot depend on Grandfather's faith any more than one can depend on Grandfather's rifle. Grandfather's faith like Grandfather's rifle served him well because he used it constantly, depended on it, practiced with it, and made it a part of everyday life. It was not an ornament and not merely a conversation piece. His attachment to it was functional, not just sentimental or intellectual. It really made a difference in his way of living.

Because of rapid changes in life-style, dependence

on technology, and a complex civilization in which we often do not see relationships between cause and effect, it is very easy for many of us in our modern world to find ourselves without a real, "working" faith. It is easy for us to allow our faith to become as the rifle on the wall—something we cherish for sentimental reasons, or enjoy for intellectual reasons (religion is as easy to argue about as an old rifle), but something that is really an antique, that does not help us get our work done and does not make a bit of difference in the way we live. It is easy to cherish because it belonged to Grandfather, but we do not use it any more than we would use any of his other tools—we have other ways of doing things now. But we have a problem. We have the same spiritual needs that Grandfather had and we need a functional faith just as much as he needed a functional rifle. We can have a working faith, but only if we have one that is our own, one we practice with and one we depend upon.

We might well ask: Is my faith truly a working faith or is it just a cherished antique like the rifle on the wall? There are ways in which we can tell if our faith really makes a difference. Do we have it on the ready and is it where we can reach it on a moment's notice? Do we instinctively reach out for it in time of trouble and when danger threatens? The frontiersman who trusted in his rifle always made sure it was where he could reach it in an instant. That is where a working faith must be. It is remarkable how many references in the Bible compare a trust in God with some form of weapon or armor. "Put on the whole armor of God" (Eph. 6:11). "The Lord is the stronghold of my life; of whom shall I be afraid?" (Ps. 27:1). Just today I was talking with an inmate of our state correctional institution. Under the guidance of a good chaplain he has become a very sincere, practicing Christian. His Christian faith is protecting him from indignities, cynicism, and the loss of a sense of personal worth—enemies that can destroy a man in prison. His life is not easy, but he looks forward to a better life on the "outside." He found his faith in the prison and he now says he is not sure whether he should say he was arrested or rescued. He is sure that his trust in God and his growing knowledge of the Christian way of life is literally his protection—his sword and his shield.

In that great story of Joseph in Egypt, Joseph could very well have been destroyed by bitterness toward his brothers. After all, they had tried to destroy him by selling him into slavery. But because of a working faith he was able to say to them: "You meant evil against me; but God meant it for good" (Gen. 50:20). His faith was where he could reach it when he needed it.

A working faith will help us understand what love is. Most of our heartache and despair, a great many of our most serious problems, social and individual, come from our failure to understand the true meaning of love. Love is the most important factor in our lives. But apart from a Christian definition, we continue to misuse the word and miss the power of real love in our lives. Our culture uses the word love in ways that at worst are pornographic and at best a simple matter of taste. I *like* ice cream but I don't *love* it. And we never know the fullness of love until we understand it in terms of our faith—until we know that love is patient and kind, that it does not seek its own way, that it is not resentful, but it bears all things and is eternal (I Cor. 13). When we learn to love, not because we desire or like someone on a human level but because we have come to know God who first loved us, then our lives can be rich and full and we can know joy and peace. Such a love does not come naturally; it is the product of a functional faith, a working relationship with One who loved the world so much that he gave his Son (John 3:16).

A working faith will provide us with guidelines for

our relationships with other people in a world where moral and ethical decisions can often be very confusing and where it is easy to get lost. In the moral teachings of Jesus we have a pole star to guide us. We do not need to stop and debate the question of right or wrong at every turn of the road. We know that truth is better than falsehood, forgiveness better than a grudge. We get the point of the story of the good Samaritan and we know that kindness is better than being mean. But we can only have the security and guidance that comes from the Christian faith if it is a "working faith"—if we have the confidence that the One who spoke the words and gave us our moral insights spoke for a God who holds the world in his hands and keeps the stars in their orbits.

The rifle that hangs on my wall is a good antique. I am glad I have it. And for me it is also a constant reminder that an antique is good to talk about and argue about but it is not adequate to live by, even if it is inherited. I want a faith that is a living faith, kept close to the areas of my life where the action is. I want a faith I can reach in an instant, a present help in the time of trouble. I want a faith that can help me know what love is and can guide me in my dealings with other people and help me make the decisions that one constantly must make.

Horse Bells

Some of my most pleasant memories are of trips that I have made in years past into primitive areas of Idaho. These trips have taken me into country far from motor roads where the means of transportation has been a good saddle horse and the means of carrying all camp gear, baggage, and meat if the trip was a hunting trip, has been the pack string, sometimes horses, generally mules. On some of these trips it has been my privilege to be in the company of a man who has had a great many years of experience with pack animals and the work that goes with handling a pack string day after day in the open country where there are no stables, corrals, or fenced pastures.

Horse Bells

For a pack string to work all day, it is necessary for them to graze a good part of the night. Among packers, the custom has developed of letting the animals loose during the night to find forage. Usually a little grain is carried along to supplement the grass the animals find, and well-trained pack animals usually learn to graze near camp, but sometimes they have to travel quite a distance to find adequate food. One of the characteristics of mules which makes it much easier for the packer to keep them together is that they become emotionally attached to a certain mare, in almost a child-parent relationship, and if the packer can keep track of the mare, he will always have his entire pack string.

When the stock is turned out to graze at night the mare has a bell put on her—she is always called the bell mare—and she, and any other horses that might have a tendency to wander or to be hard to catch in the morning, are hobbled. Horse hobbles are a painless arrangement something like a set of handcuffs that simply fasten the horse's front feet together so she can travel with very small steps or hops, but cannot run. Usually the bell mare is quite a favorite with the packer, something of a pet who gets good treatment and often a very light load to carry—perhaps some of the light camping equipment. The mules, who will not leave the bell mare, are allowed to run loose while they graze.

Every experienced packer will have a fine bell of his own for his bell mare. He will know the tone of his bell; it will be a bell one can hear for quite a distance, and he will generally claim his bell to be of better tone and quality than others. He prizes it, and unless through some misfortune he has lost it, probably has a bell that he has prized for many years.

One of the memories that I have, and really cherish, is of the many peaceful nights I have spent with my good friend out in the back country with camp set up, horses and mules turned out to graze, supper finished, lying in a warm sleeping bag waiting for sleep to come and listening to the steady, musical ring of the horse bell while the pack string grazed near camp. One could almost feel the peace and quiet of the vast open country with the only sounds being the ringing of the bell and the other night sounds of the forest. A light breeze makes a music of its own in the trees; sometimes a night bird calls; occasionally a coyote will give an answering call to the ring of the horse bell.

Almost everyone who has had experience packing in wild country agrees that of all the bell sounds in the world—striking clocks, church bells, engine bells on trains—there is no sweeter, better sound than the music of horse bells. Of course, one of the reasons a packer loves the sound of a horse bell is that the steady ringing tells him that all is well. The animals are where they are supposed to be; they are grazing near camp, have found good feed, and the packer is free to relax and get his much-needed rest.

As much as I have enjoyed the sound of horse bells, not being a very good sleeper, the ringing has had a tendency to keep me awake. I have spent many pleasant, but wakeful, hours listening to the bell and thinking long thoughts. This has given me an opportunity to observe my friend, who is experienced with outdoor living and has spent hundreds of nights sleeping to the music of the horse bells. I learned quite early that he could drop right off to sleep with the bell ringing. But if the bell would stop ringing for awhile he would wake up. And if it did not ring for several minutes, he would say, "Our stock must have strayed and are getting too far from camp. We'd better get up and check on them, or we may have a long hunt for them in the morning." We would get up, locate the pack string, bring them back nearer camp, and tie up the bell mare till morning. I have been fascinated by this ability to relax and sleep contentedly while a bell is ringing, and then wake up when the bell stops ringing, realizing that the quietness is a sign of trouble.

There is something about horse bells that makes me think of the function of a Christian's conscience. Christianity sets some pretty high standards for us to live by—high standards of moral and ethical conduct. It is our awareness of these standards and our effort to live by them to the best of our ability that can give us the good life we all seek. The sound of a bell is normally, and rightly, thought of as a disturbing sound. If our conscience is properly trained and disciplined in the Christian faith, we will live best when the moral principles of our faith keep some bells ringing— keeping us aware of the fact that we are not as good as we ought to be and aware of the fact that it is not easy to live a Christian life in a culture that is quite indifferent to much that is of great importance in the Christian life. One does not need to recite the evidence of the lack of moral standards in our society. The news keeps us aware of it: business and political dishonesty, broken homes, personal disillusionment on every hand as people have tried to live without moral standards.

There should be something about the very character of a church that disturbs us as we walk into a service of worship. If our conscience is working right we will find ourselves saying, God, be merciful to me a sinner. There should be something disturbing about Christian preaching as it seeks to keep us aware of the life and teachings of Jesus, who talked a good deal about the values that make life worthwhile and asked, What does it profit a man to gain the world and lose his soul? As Christians we certainly cannot take our moral standards from the world in which we live. There are ways of life to which we must not adjust even if "everyone is doing it." When Paul said, "Don't let the world around you squeeze you into its own mould'' (Rom. 12:2, Phillips), he certainly was speaking to the twentieth-century Christian. And the world will squeeze into its own mold everyone it can, and it certainly will do it to anyone who does not have a clear-cut standard of right and wrong and a conscience that is sensitive enough to keep him aware of situations that are not as they ought to be; a conscience so sensitive that he will wake up if he doesn't hear the bell.

It is a bitter experience to wake up in camp in the morning and find that the pack animals have wandered away while you slept and what was to have been a pleasant day is spent in a long difficult hike, tracking the strayed animals and bringing them back to camp. And all is the result of your being content to sleep long after the sound of the horse bell had grown faint in the distance and finally stopped ringing altogether. It is a much more bitter experience to wake up in life and find that you have allowed your conscience to become dull and sleepy. The bells of your moral standards have grown faint and finally stopped sounding altogether and while you slept all that you have really cherished—the love of a good family, the respect of your business associates, your ability to be a good influence in politics—all these have walked away in the night and you never realized that the failure to hear the bells meant that there would be trouble in the morning.

My friend who can relax and sleep to the sound of the bell on the bell mare has a very fine bell. He is proud of it and I am sure he would not sell it for any price. It is his bell, and I know that one of the reasons it means so much to him is that it was given to him by his father.

Cleaning Ditches

All my life I have been involved to some extent with the process of irrigation. Webster defines irrigate: "To supply land with water by causing a stream to flow upon, over or through it. . . ." I have known some of my deepest satisfactions by being a part of this process. I have spent almost all of my life in Idaho, a state famous for its crops of potatoes, sugar beets, beans, sweet corn, and fruit. These crops grow in abundance in addition to a fine livestock industry that depends on irrigated hay and pasture land. All of this is produced in a state where most of the good farmlands are found in areas classified as desert on the basis of the amount of rainfall. These lands remain desert unless touched by the magic of irrigation.

The Snake River and its tributaries are to the life and economy of Idaho what the blood stream is to a human body. To one who enjoys seeing things grow, there is a strange joy in the process of irrigating—causing a stream of water to flow upon the land. It is almost as if one is sharing with God in the process of creation. Perhaps he is; this may be the reason it brings a real joy. When I was a boy I used to help my father irrigate potato fields. When the vines covered the little streams that ran between the rows, I would stay at one end of the field and with a system of signals indicate to Dad the rows in which the water had reached the end of the field so he could readjust the flow into the rows needing more water. What a joy for a barefooted boy to be able to play in the water, squish his toes in the mud, and be doing something useful at the same time.

In our irrigated country, the water is shut out of the canals and ditches during the winter and turned back in as the irrigation season approaches in the spring. A part of my springtime experience has always been the spring cleaning of the ditches that carry water to the fields. Some ditches require more cleaning than others. But no matter how well a ditch is engineered or how well it is managed it requires some cleaning. Silt, debris, last year's weeds or leaves, erosion caused by animals— there is always something that will need to be cleaned out or repaired before the ditch will carry its maximum flow. Keeping some ditches in repair can be very hard work.

A certain ditch at Sky Range Ranch came directly out of the creek that flows through the ranch. It came on grade around the side of a hill and delivered water to two small mountain meadows. When it first left the creek it flowed through woods. It had been built many years ago with a horse-drawn plow. Trees had grown on the banks, and it was impossible to get a tractor or other modern machinery in to "plow" the ditch, so I always cleaned it by the old-fashioned method—simply taking my shovel and going along the length of the ditch to clean it out. This can be very hard work, but it requires almost no intelligence. One can keep one's body employed while the mind is free to do all sorts of things. In our complex modern society I think we all might be better off with more of this sort of work. I always came away from a day of cleaning that ditch with a weary body and a much refreshed mind.

The woods through which the ditch ran made it a pleasant place to work, but greatly increased the work. Added to the grass and weeds I found in other ditches on the ranch was the crop of leaves from the trees in the woods. Nothing plugs up a ditch faster than last summer's leaves. Deer lived in the woods, and their trails broke down the ditch bank. My cattle liked the woods in winter and added their share of innocent destruction. And some summers I even had a pair of beavers who liked to alter the entire flow with an experimental dam. The same trees that filled my ditch with leaves did give me pleasant shade to work in and the deer that broke my ditch banks never ceased to be a source of pleasure—I met them often enough that I knew them as individuals. And I shall never forget the day an embarrassed beaver tried to hide himself by going to the very bottom of the ditch—sixteen inches of crystal clear water.

Cleaning ditches seems to me to be similar to the exercise of the Christian life. How often the love of God has been compared, and rightly so, to a stream of life-giving water. God gives his love freely, even as the snow melts on the mountains and the streams flow freely toward the sea. To the Christian there is given the challenge of being a channel for God's love. We do our part to cause it to "flow upon, over, and through" a parched and thirsty world. I have reflected on this as I have done my spring cleaning and thought how much my own life is like that ditch through the woods.

Often in summer when I have had the ditch flowing full at evening time, I have gone back in the morning to check on it, only to find a break in the bank, and the stream flowing uselessly back to the creek. I have learned the hard way that there is no use trying to repair the break until I have gone the length of the ditch and cleaned out the trash or debris that has blocked the flow and caused the water to break out of its banks and run to no purpose, or worse, to cause damaging erosion. How often this happens in other areas of life. The channels of goodwill and love that should be flowing between me and other members of the family, or my fellow workers, or neighbors, are broken. It seems that life is running to no good purpose. And I find that no matter how hard I try to mend the break in the ditch bank, I cannot until I first go the length of the ditch, and find the place where the debris of trivia has accumulated to block the channel, or the silt of indifference or the mud of selfishness has accumulated until the flow of water has been reduced to a dribble. Only after I have cleaned, widened, and deepened the whole channel of my life can I repair the particular break in communication that has been causing my trouble.

We cannot keep the water of life flowing through a channel that is blocked by trash. We cannot repair the broken places until the trash is cleaned out. And for the very reason that the ditch of my life flows through woods where there are living things—the work of cleaning it is never finished. I can never fix it once and for all, any more than I can save my soul, or say my prayers, or give my love once and for all. Every summer brings its new crop of leaves and weeds; each fall the cattle come off the hills, and any night the beavers may move in. While there is life I shall be cleaning ditches—mending broken places, cleaning out trash. It is hard work. But I shall also know the joy of seeing dry land turned into green pastures and desert places producing crops for hungry people.

Without A Lead Rope

He leads me beside still waters. . . . in paths of righteousness. . . . Even though I walk through the valley of the shadow of death, I fear no evil.

—Psalm 23:2b-4a

I have always been interested in the idea of leading and being led; there are so many different ways of leading, so many different reasons for following. Perhaps my interest in leading comes from my own deep need to be led or guided by One who is wiser and braver than I. Perhaps it comes partly from the fact that I have had the role of leadership with people to some small extent as I have tried to be a good pastor. Also, I

36

have had a good deal of experience in the leading of animals—horses and mules. I do not want to push comparisons too far, but there are some fascinating comparisons that can be made from experience with quiet animals (I prefer the term *quiet animal* to *dumb animal* because we often use the word dumb to mean something quite different than the simple inability to speak and communicate with words, and my animals are not dumb in the sense of being stupid). Throughout Scripture we find interesting comparisons between sheep and people in terms of their need for being led, so I risk the comparison in terms of some of the other quiet animals.

For many years one of my favorite forms of recreation has been travel into the rugged, roadless areas of our state by saddle horse. If the trip has been a fairly long one, such as a hunting trip, with the prospect of bringing home an elk or a deer, or even a fishing trip to a mountain lake where I will want my rubber raft, my tent, and other things that make for a good camp, there has generally been the need to lead one or more pack animals.

Leading a pack animal that is not well trained can be an exasperating experience. Perhaps your saddle horse is a bit eager and the pack animal is always hanging back, which means the hand that holds the lead rope can be sore and tired by the end of the day. Sometimes your shoulder can be really hurt when your saddle horse crosses a log or stream quickly and the stubborn pack animal balks or "sets back," giving you a choice of dropping the lead rope or getting a pretty nasty jerk or a rope burn as the slack is pulled from your grasp.

If you have a good saddle horse who knows his business and has worked a rope, there is a temptation to tie "hard and fast." This means tying the pack animal's lead rope to your saddle horn so that when the pack animal lags or sets back, the shock is taken by your saddle horse who has the strength to handle it and instead of your losing the rope or getting a sore arm, the stubborn or balky pack mule may get a sore nose. There is hazard in tying hard and fast and every good cowboy or packer knows the hazard. The pack animal is strong and if tied hard and fast, he may, in some moment of foolishness or fear, be able to pull both you and your saddle horse off balance, perhaps off the trail and over a steep embankment or cliff. There have been good men and good horses killed simply because they were tied hard and fast to a mean, stupid, or panic-stricken pack animal.

If you have a really fine rope horse and the country is not too rough, you can compromise with what we call a dally. You take a wrap or two of rope, the dally, around your saddle horn, giving yourself a great deal more ability to hold the lead rope because of the friction of the rope on the saddle horn. Yet in a time of emergency it does come loose, and you can be free of the lead rope. However, even this has its hazards in rough country. A gloved hand can be caught in the dally; a finger can be broken; or, if a dally binds too tightly, a good rope horse can still be jerked unmercifully and, on a bad trail, dangerously.

When you lead a string of pack animals, of course, you only lead the first one, and if the string is tied together, the wise packer ties each animal to the one ahead of it with the lead rope attached to a small piece of much lighter rope that will break before it will pull an animal off the trail. But even this system has some problems. There are cases of pack animals being injured by being pulled off the trail by another animal which lost its footing, panicked, or balked.

The only reason for using a lead rope on a pack animal is that the animal is not sufficiently trained. He has not been used enough to know to follow in his place in the string without a lead rope. He has not been following his leader and master enough to know to follow by habit and his own willingness, realizing that he is much safer and his work is easier if he follows willingly, rather than being led by an uncompromising lead rope that forces him to do what he ought to do of his own will.

In years past when the pack train was the only way of moving freight in many parts of the country, pack animals were used so regularly and it was such a daily part of their lives, that most of the old-time packers could let their animals follow without a lead rope, and this was a much more satisfactory way to handle them. The well-trained mule knew his place in the string, would stand in the morning by his own pack and harness, in the very place it was unloaded the night before, and, because of his trust, training, and dependability, the entire task was made easier for the packer and the animals involved. Only occasionally does one see such a pack string in modern times, because it does take a great deal of time and work together to develop this quality of trust and dependability in a pack string. There are a few that work enough to achieve it in our time, and it is a joy to behold. Pack animals that can be trusted to follow without a lead rope and a packer who knows he can trust his animals in this way can accomplish a good deal more in a day, and with much less hazard, effort, and hard work, than is possible in an untrained, undisciplined string that must always be led and sometimes tied hard and fast.

One of my favorite scriptures is the simple phrase from Psalm 23 that says, "He leads me." He leads me in the very places I should go—the places that will make my life productive and secure. He leads me by still water, in green pastures, and through the dark and possibly frightening valley of the shadow. But having done some packing, with various animals, whenever I read the phrase "He leads me," I want to add the words "without a lead rope"! He doesn't drag me against my will; I am sure if I resist and he needs to snub me with a mule halter and tie hard and fast to hang onto me, I will never see the green of the pastures anyhow or taste the still waters. One of the most appealing parts of the Twenty-third Psalm is a sense of gentleness: the picture of one being led, but without any force applied. He is being led only because he is very willing to follow in complete trust.

To me, this picture of our relationship to God is very important. God never forces us against our will. We have loads to carry and long trails to travel. But we have learned, like the good pack animal, that we can trust the one who leads; following him we will come at evening time to the campsite where the grass is good and the water sweet and cool. We have learned that by following gladly we get early into camp, with time to have our sore backs anointed, our tired feet checked, and our shoes reset if they are causing us trouble. We have found we can carry a heavier, more useful load over a difficult trail if we are not having to worry about, or fight with, a confining lead rope, but can have some discretion in picking our pace, taking our own time in getting over a log or a bad rock in the trail. And we are fortunate if we learn in our youth that stubbornly to refuse to follow unless we are pulled by a lead rope simply increases our labors, greatly increases the dangers of stumbling with our load, and, at best, brings us into camp at night with a sore nose.

The Dogs of God

Goodness and mercy shall follow me all the days of my life; and I will dwell in the house of the Lord for ever.

—Psalm 23:6 (KJV)

A few years ago I was riding my horse through some high, brushy, mountain rangeland. It was rough country, and much of the brush was nearly as high as the back of my horse. There were a few small clumps of trees, but, in general, from the height of my saddle, I could see for a good long way. From a ridgetop I could see for several miles. It was quite early in the morning, and I came upon a band of sheep—perhaps a thousand

ewes—with their lambs. The sheep were feeding and
slowly moving in one general direction at the same
time. The brush was high enough that I knew a sheep
could not see over it, and yet the band was staying
together rather well and I noticed the herder sitting
under a tree on a little rise where he could keep
everything in view. I marvelled at how well they stayed
together, and I was interested in the herder's calmness
and lack of concern. I was sure that in his place I would
have been very concerned lest the sheep get hopelessly
scattered and lost in the brushy, uneven country. Then I
saw something fascinating, and I knew why the herder
was not upset and why the sheep grazed in security.
The herder had two large, intelligent, powerful dogs.
The dogs were constantly on the alert, instantly ready
to put back in the flock any ewe or lamb that strayed too
far. Part of the time the dogs were simply patrolling the
edge of the herd; part of the time they were resting
beside the herder but ready on a moment's notice to
respond to his command and "shape up" any section of
the flock that might be getting a little too ambitious in
their grazing and too far out of touch with the main
body of sheep. Generally the dogs put a ewe back in her
place quite gently, but they could be pretty rough if need
be. They had teeth, and they knew how to use them on
the heels of a stubborn sheep, though nearly always just
the presence of the dog or a little bark of warning was
all that any sheep needed to keep her safely in her place
in the grazing flock.

It is a joy to watch a good sheep dog working under
difficult circumstances such as I saw on that range. The
dog combines desire and talents in the instinct born of
centuries of good breeding and hours and hours of
patient training. Next to the herder himself, the dog is
by far the most important security that the sheep has.
Yet I have a feeling that if you could talk to the average
sheep, she would say she really didn't care for sheep

dogs—too fussy, too bossy, and sometimes downright mean.

I stopped to visit with the herder. He bragged on the quality of his dogs (all herders either believe they have the finest dogs in the world or get rid of them and get better ones), and, as the morning wore on, the sheep began to finish their grazing and lie down. The dogs saw to it that by the time the sheep were lying down they were all bunched and accounted for, and it was then time for herder and dogs to relax and have a good nap before the evening grazing began. I rode on my way, but I rode on with much to think about. I had a whole new insight into the meaning of the great shepherd psalm, Psalm 23.

Life in this world is a fine adventure. There are green pastures to graze, interesting places to explore, and sometimes dark valleys to cross. And we humans are able to enjoy the adventure, to find the good pastures and the still waters, because, even though we are not as wise as we ought to be, there is a good shepherd who cares for us, and he has a couple of dogs. Their names are Goodness and Mercy, and they dog our heels from the time we are first turned out on the range until at last we find our way over the last high ridge into that green valley called the "house of the Lord" where we are no longer in danger and can dwell in safety forever.

One of the most important contributions of the Christian faith is that it makes us aware that life is good, but not the final good. Our life on this earth is much like the summer season for the sheep in the beautiful high country ranges of Idaho. It is beautiful and good, but temporary. Life is a pilgrimage. It is a constant journey. It is a summer's grazing and growing on a good range, but our final destiny is not the green pasture, or the still water, or the dark valley—it is the house of the Lord for ever, and until we reach it the dogs of God will be at our heels, watching us, correcting us, guiding us—sometimes having to get pretty rough with us, and never letting us "settle down" in a permanent way in this life.

The good, the bad, the beautiful, the ugly, the joy, the sorrow—all are part of this life and all are temporary. Our final home is otherwhere and we go as those who seek a city whose maker and builder is God.

One of the greatest causes of unrest, frustration, and at times fanaticism and cruelty, is man's failure to recognize the temporary nature of this life and his efforts to treat this life as if it were the final good. In his search for a perfect society and in his assurance that his way is the right way, man is at times willing even to kill his neighbor, or to put him in a concentration camp, or to deny him his normal rights. He does these foolish things because he thinks he is dealing with a society that can be a "good society," that the end justifies the means, and that those who stand in his way are to be eliminated. How important it is to remember that life is good, but not the final good, and a society or culture really has no more permanence than the individuals who comprise it. When we know we cannot store permanent treasures on earth, either as personal belongings or as a classless society or as a "kingdom of God," then we can afford to love our neighbors, forgive those who trespass against us, and pray for those who despitefully use us.

In his book *Future Shock,* Alvin Toffler speaks of the shock that comes upon us when we find that things are constantly changing and at an accelerating speed. He speaks of "the death of permanence." But of course, the Christian is not shocked for he has always known there is no permanence in this life. The apostle Paul was 1900 years ahead of Toffler with this important insight. In our recent political interest in wilderness preservation we have developed a propaganda slogan which refers to wilderness areas as places where man is only a visitor. But it is high time that we remember that this is true of all of life in this world. In the sight of God there is really not that much difference between a day or a week or eighty years, and in this life man is always a visitor, always a sheep grazing on a summer range, and the dogs of God will never let him settle down for very long in one place.

Sometimes the dogs of God come to us in ways we do not like. We are following our own inclinations. We think we have found a delightful meadow where we will just stay while the rest of the flock moves on. But just when we think we are established and have it all to ourselves, the Goodness and Mercy of God will come nipping at our heels and we will have to move on and take our place with the rest of the sheep that move along toward summer's end and experiences that are beyond the next ridge. Sometimes we have seen what we thought were greener pastures away from the plans of the Good Shepherd, and what we thought was hard luck, lack of money, sickness, aging, or some other mortal problem has barred the way and kept us from doing what we wanted to do. We were angry and resentful, and perhaps stubborn. The dogs showed their teeth and it was hard for us to recognize them as goodness and mercy. We would have called them something else—maybe pain or grief.

Real love is not always gentle and soft but pushes us in the way that we have to go. An old cowboy friend told me a gruesome story of his early experience on the ranges of southern Idaho. He and his companion were caught in a bitter winter storm. His companion was not as hardy as Jim; nor was he as well dressed for the cruel weather. He became so cold that he decided to give up and lie down. Jim knew that if his companion did what he wanted to do—stop walking and lie down in the snow—it would be only a few minutes before he would freeze to death. Taking away the man's gun so he could not defend himself, Jim proceeded to use his drover's whip to literally whip the man the remaining miles into camp. It was harsh, but it saved his life and in time—it took awhile—the man thanked him for it.

Sometimes the dogs of God must use their teeth on us. When we think we have it made in this life and want to rest and settle for the values of this world, forgetting that we are pilgrims, not settlers, these strong, capable dogs will hound us.

There is an old law of trespass which stated that if any animal remained for twenty-four hours on the land of someone other than his owner, he would become the property of the one on whose land he remained. Some of the property of this world may belong to us for awhile, but when we become so interested in the things of this world that we want to stay forever in it, Goodness and Mercy dog our heels and move us on toward our final dwelling place, making sure we do not remain long enough in this world to become its property. No matter how much we may dislike being driven by the dogs of God, the day will come when we will look back from a better world than this and be glad that we were not always allowed to follow our own whims. We will be glad that Goodness and Mercy followed us, at times guided us, and when necessary drove us, all the days of our lives.

Vine & Fig Tree

They shall sit every man under his vine and under his fig tree, and none shall make them afraid.

—Micah 4:4

Being country people, when my wife and I moved to town we had to bring some of the country with us. We live in an area where most of the families have more than an acre and our two-and-one-half acre lot is rather typical. It is an area where there are still fence rows, irrigation ditches, weed patches. Many wild creatures thrive now even more than they did when the land was more closely cropped as part of a larger farm. My neighbor tells me my place is too large for a hoe and too small for a tractor. Except for a small vegetable garden and some flower beds, our farming is very inefficient and limited to raising a little pasture for our horses. But we have our rewards. We eat our meals beside a window from which we see all sorts of wonderful sights in our back yard. Perhaps the foals are racing each other around the pasture, or a mother pheasant is looking for a place to put her nest. Perhaps some migrating birds have stopped for a brief rest and are refueling on the seeds of our weeds. The scene changes with the seasons; it is always a source of joy and wonder. Our window is a viewing screen for a great deal that is fundamental to the whole world of nature. I am glad I am healthy and can go places and do things, but if my view of the world were limited to that which I can see from our window, I would still have a vast and wonderful world to learn from and wonder about. I am quite sure that one can see more by looking closely and with awe at a very small part of creation than one can by traveling thousands of miles and looking quickly and thoughtlessly at a vast number of different scenes to which one has no intimate relationship.

On one particular bright spring morning as we ate our breakfast we were treated to a special bit of pageantry. It was as new as each spring morning and as old as creation—a little drama that gives us an insight into the very nature of created life including our own human nature with its needs and hopes, dreams and disappointments. On our back lawn a meadowlark in all his bright spring finery, dressed in his courting clothes, was preening and strutting about in such a confident manner that it was plain to see he really thought he owned the place. He had "staked his claim" to the little bit of territory that I had thought was my lawn, but he was perfectly sure it was his place.

He does not know that the territory he has claimed is our yard, and it is good he doesn't, because his very survival, his future, his part in the ongoing life of his species, depends on his complete confidence that this is his yard. His confidence is contagious and gives him strength and security. He is so confident that his title, by right of discovery, is an insurable title that he can defeat any other male meadowlark that comes along. And because he is a landowner and has securities, he is confident that a charming lady will look on him with approval and come to share his life and be co-owner of his bit of real estate. Of course, he is exactly right. This is just what happens, and before long it will be papa and mama and little meadowlarks that own our yard, and we will mow the lawn and tend the garden carefully so as not to offend them unduly by trespassing on "private property."

Watching our meadowlark strut his stuff has added a delight to our breakfast, and I leave for the office with much to think about. I am reminded again that an all-wise Creator has designed both meadowlarks and men so that they must have certain securities in life, certain things they can believe and certain places to which they belong. For the meadowlark this is a matter of instinct—he does not have to reason it out or think about it. For man it is more complicated. He can think about it, talk with his neighbors about his beliefs, make some deliberate choices about his life-style. The meadowlark cannot deny his basic nature and survive. Either he becomes involved, attached, finds a territory that is his, accepts it and defends it, or he does not mate, and probably does not survive the season. Man, intellectually, can deny his nature. He can try to live without roots, without loyalties, without a sense of belonging to a community, family, or church. But I am convinced that he can deny his nature only for a while and cannot survive well as an individual, and not at all as a species, unless he accepts that part of his nature that requires the putting down of roots. For man, this does not mean he must always live in one place, or live with one set of ideas. There must be adventure, a willingness to innovate. It does mean there is an acceptance of loyalties, the ability to say with sincerity and a sense of obligation: This is my home, this is my husband or this is my wife, this is my country, this is my duty. Our biblical faith urges us constantly to be moving on seeking a better way, but the very challenge to move forward in our beliefs implies that we have had a base from which to move. One cannot make a leap forward without having a firm footing from which to leap. It is my conviction that a great deal of the anxiety, frustration, and violence in our society is a result of the rootlessness of our way of life. Most personal or social problems involve people who have an anxiety that is not specific, but is fear born of insecurity—the kind of insecurity that is the direct result of not having a sense of belonging. A great insight of the prophet Micah is the realization that it is when man has found a homeland, when he has his own vine and fig tree—his place, where he belongs and is someone—it is then, and only then, that "none shall make him afraid."

I am certainly not a trained biologist, but some of the findings about the concept of the "territorial imperative" seem to have important implications for our own human lives. In the animal world we see this need for a place in an elemental form. All species apparently indicate the need, and we are finding that the need for attachment to a place, the security of one's own niche in the scheme of things, is even more basic than the mating urge and that mating depends on it. With man, this basic need is more than simply the need for a physical territory, though we should not play down the importance of having a place we can call our own. But in human beings the need might best be described as the willingness to be involved and obligated: to be willing to own your home and pay your taxes, marry your mate and be loyal to him or her, join your church and pay your share of its support. Having your place, your "vine and fig tree," is part of being yourself. It may be a ranch house, it may be a nice home in the suburbs, it may be a small rented apartment, but it is your place. You can choose the curtains and you can light a candle on the dinner table. You can close the door when you wish, and you can open it to whom you wish.

In this brief chapter I can speak only of a feeling; I cannot get involved in a deep study of this human need that is part of our nature. Paul Tournier has an excellent discussion of it in his fine book *A Place For You,* and his first chapter, "Somewhere To Be," touches the heart of the longing that we all have for "our place." But on this particular spring morning I am grateful to my friend the meadowlark who reminded me so well that a very real part of life is knowing who we are and where we live and being willing to accept the obligations and rewards that go along with being someone and having somewhere to be. As I watched the pretty fellow so proudly claiming my yard as his territory I was glad that his place and my place can be the same place.

Beyond
the First
Range of Hills

Our daughters are interested in endurance riding, an increasingly popular sport among horsemen who like to ride good horses over long and difficult mountain trails. Perhaps the best known of these rides is the Tevis Cup ride that starts near Lake Tahoe on the California-Nevada border, crosses the rugged crest of the Sierra-Nevada range on the old Pony Express trail, and after one hundred extremely rugged miles ends at the fair grounds at Auburn, California. Another well-known hundred-mile ride begins and ends at Virginia City, Nevada. We have accompanied our youngest daughter, Heidi, and her beloved stallion, Surrabu, to both of these rides and several others and have found that it is an interesting way to meet new people and see new country. Being from Idaho we naturally have suggested from time to time that it would be great to have a hundred-mile ride somewhere in our state. I was amazed on one occasion when I suggested this to have the person respond by asking, "Is there anywhere in Idaho where we could find a trail that would be scenic, and steep enough to really test the horses?"

Having spent much of my life in central Idaho, which includes the nations three deepest canyons and is for the most part fantastically beautiful, my first reaction to this person's question was one of unbelief. How could anyone know anything at all about Idaho and think that it might lack steep mountains and beautiful scenery. Then, on second thought, I realized it could be possible and on asking the person about his experience in Idaho I found that it was as I suspected. The main highway crossing southern Idaho, approximately on the route of the old Oregon Trail, crosses for the most part the one fairly flat area in the entire state—the Snake River Plain. If one crosses on Interstate 80, and crosses pretty fast, one can get the impression that Idaho is a predominantly flat, sagebrush-covered state with a few farms and, in the distance, on either side of the valley, a low range of hills. When the highway is close to the low foothills, these hills themselves can block out the view of the ranges of mountains that lie beyond, though on a clear day you can generally see some of the peaks that lie beyond the first range of hills. But without stopping to think about it, one might very well limit one's view of the state to the flat places and the first range of low hills. We lived for awhile right in the mountains, in a little cabin so sheltered by low hills that unless one left the cabin and got away from the front door, one might never know one was surrounded by towering peaks and great snow-covered ridges. It is very easy to let your view be limited by the low hills in the immediate foreground and miss the greatest scenery in the world.

We are all inclined to do this in our daily life. We let our view be limited by the edge of the little materialistic valley where we live. The sun rises and sets on the rim of the low hills just outside our window, and unless we make some effort to cultivate the spirit, to exercise the mind, to stretch the imagination, we can find ourselves believing there is nothing more to life than the little hills that surround the valley where we live and work.

Jesus told us a story about a rich farmer who put all his effort into material gain, building bigger barns, only to find that this life was a dead-end street and there were more important things to do than making a killing in investments. The farmer had limited his view of life to the first range of low hills. In the game of life the clock is always running. That's what makes it interesting. And that's what makes it worthwhile to give some thought to the high and beautiful scenery that lies beyond the immediate foreground.

A few years ago a man sold me some mortgage insurance. I said I would buy it and then, just to cover his bets, he said he wanted a doctor to examine me. I submitted to the poking and prying, and when it was all over the doctor said he thought I might live another ten years, so the insurance company put up some pretty good stakes betting that I might, and I put up my premiums as my stakes, betting that I might not. I hope the insurance company is right. But let's suppose the doctor had been a real wizard and been able to say, with certainty, that I am a bad bet and will die in the next two years. What would I do?

Well, first of all I think I would try to get a better look at what I feel sure lies beyond the next range of hills, and I hope that wouldn't be too different from what I am trying to do now. I would want to love my loves with added tenderness and concern, being more sensitive to their feelings. I would try to live with more awareness and appreciation of the good earth. This world and this life are much too wonderful to be taken for granted. I would cry out with Edna St. Vincent Millay: "O world, I cannot hold thee close enough!"

I would want to take a closer look at the chrysanthemums that are blooming in our back yard, the ones my wife has tended so carefully and which I have almost mowed down a time or two. I would want to study the dainty leaves of the little black birches that we transplanted from the creek that runs through the ranch where we used to live. I would spend more time studying the flowing motion of the young colt that runs in the pasture—running for the pure joy of running and as a celebration of the warm young life within him. I would go ahead with the hunting trip I'm planning to take this fall, but I would care less whether or not I got an elk and would take more pleasure in studying the animal tracks, smelling the morning breeze when it blows up from the creek bottom as the sun warms the air. I would take along on my hunting trip a little Bible, and maybe sit in the sun on a ridge at noontime and read:

Bless the Lord . . .
who hast stretched out the heavens like a tent, . . .
who makest the clouds thy chariot,
   who ridest on the wings of the wind, . . .
Thou makest springs gush forth in the valleys;
   they flow between the hills,
they give drink to every beast of the field; . . .
Thou dost cause the grass to grow for the cattle,
   and plants for man to cultivate, . . .
The high mountains are for the wild goats;
   the rocks are a refuge for the badgers.
Thou hast made the moon to mark the seasons.
                   (Ps. 104:1-19*a*)

55

I would love with more sensitivity the earth that God has created.

I would love my church, my scriptures, my Jesus, with more intensity. I would try to be a better preacher, but would also try to spend more time with my wife and family, especially my grandchildren. And then, I would want to do with my life what I try to do with my writing. I would try to edit out the trivia.

It is easier to write a five-thousand-word essay than a five-hundred-word essay because in the longer one you have room for more irrelevant thoughts and words that lack sharp, clear meaning. With five hundred words to cover a subject you really have to fry the fat out of every sentence. In an essay you cannot edit in greatness but you can edit out the trivial. With the shortness of life I surely want to use the blue pencil and edit out all grudges, hatreds, and feelings of remorse or resentment. I once heard of a man who, because of things that happened in the early years of his marriage, spent fifty years resenting his wife's side of the family. He made a special effort to make sure none of them inherited any of his estate. What a waste of time and space in the essay of life.

How do we edit out trivia? In a manuscript we do it by always keeping in mind what we really want to say and ruthlessly marking out what is pointless. In life, this might mean staying home from a board meeting and helping a granddaughter take care of a pet lamb. With a manuscript, you write it and let it cool a few days, and then, with a more objective view, you can see the phrases and words that don't add a bit to the meaning. In life, this is one of the functions of prayer. At the end of the day you quietly reread the day's activities in the presence of God, and you can see the things that have added nothing to the meaning and might just as well be edited out of tomorrow's plans. It is when we look at life from God's point of view knowing that "a thousand years in his sight are but as yesterday when it is past, or as a watch in the night" (Ps. 90:4) that we can keep the trivial from obscuring that which has real meaning. When we truly come to know that he has been "our dwelling place in all generations" (Ps. 90:1), we can get above and beyond the first range of hills limiting our view and narrowing the valley where we live and see that "from everlasting to everlasting" the mountains of his love and mercy stretch out before us and that our little world fits into his great world in the way that it should.

Who Did the Dishes?

Many times over the years of my life as a pastor I have celebrated the Communion service with my congregation. It has been my privilege and responsibility to conduct the service and serve the bread and wine. As I move along the Communion rail, serving the bits of bread and the little wine cups, I do not see the faces of the people who kneel there. But I see the hands that reach out to take the sacred symbols. There is such a story in hands that I hope God will forgive me when I sometimes allow my mind to wander and wonder about the hands, when perhaps I should have my mind on other things.

Who Did the Dishes?

Hands tell a wonderful story of the common tasks of life. I have spent most of my ministry in communities where there were many farmers and ranchers, loggers and miners, as well as business men and women. Perhaps there was a wider variety of hands in the rural community than in my present parish where most of the people are more closely related to the business world. But there is still a wonderful variety of hands though they now may tell me more about the owner's hobby than his or her daily work.

Hands show our age, and one of the strengths of the church is the fact there is no generation gap—a young hand reaches up beside an old hand. Here is a hand, well scrubbed, but it cannot deny the fact that for five days a week it has been taking apart and putting back together automobile engines. Here is a nicely kept hand but the nail on one finger is black from a misguided hammer on a Saturday hobby job. Here is a hand twisted with arthritis and another that has been, some time in the past, too close to a table saw. I see the hands; I ponder the truth of our faith that speaks of "varieties of gifts, but the same Spirit; and there are varieties of service, but the same Lord" (I Cor. 12:4-5).

Because of my country background, when I think of variety of service, my mind turns to tasks like cultivating crops, flaking baled hay out for hungry cattle, baking bread, washing dishes and making beds, and holding crying babies. I think of hands that have lovingly served the church by volunteer work, putting shingles on a leaking roof or painting the Sunday school rooms or laying carpet in a hallway. I sometimes think of talented hands that play the organ or direct a choir, but the word "service" brings up first in my own mind physical, manual, and what we sometimes think of as menial labor. As the Communion service proceeds, my mind keeps running back to the beginnings of the sacrament and the dinner that Jesus shared with his disciples. We generally speak of it as the "Last Supper." In my Communion meditation I have reflected on what this supper must have meant to our Lord and what the symbolic supper must mean to me as I am asked to share it in remembrance of him. What grief and concern must have been upon him; what common human sadness as he shared the meal with those he had learned to love, knowing it would be the last time they would sit down to the table together and feel the warmth of fellowship that comes from a shared meal.

The service is over and the symbolic bread and wine is back on the altar table where I cover it with a cloth and prepare to go my way. But almost always at this point in the service a haunting question comes to me. I know who will take care of the Communion things in our church. We have a devoted member of the congregation who will clean them and lovingly put them away until another day. But at that Last Supper which was the first Communion, it was not quite that simple; it was not all organized as it is today. After supper Jesus and his disciples left and went out in the night to the Mount of Olives to pray. But who stayed behind and did the dishes? What faithful person did this common task? We have always been so concerned, and rightly so, with the great events following the Last Supper that we have never thought much about this unknown person or persons whose faithful work and dedicated efforts made possible the comfort and provided for the needs of our Lord on that very difficult night.

Perhaps it was the man or the wife of the man whom Jesus speaks of in Mark 14 when he asks his disciples to prepare for the passover and tells them to go into the city where they will find a man carrying a water jar. They are to follow him and find the guest room prepared and ready, "as he had told them." What a joy this must have been to Jesus when tired, burdened with the concerns that were upon him, to arrive and find the room prepared. What if he had arrived and it had not been prepared; if the dishes from last night's supper were still in the sink? What if no one had swept the floor and the place had been a mess? And what if Jesus had asked. "Why is the room not ready?" and been told, "We were interested in more spiritual things. We want to know more about your philosophy and the prophecies. We have been reading the scriptures. We have no time for common things like cooking and sweeping and doing dishes."

As I read and reread the teaching of Jesus I find more and more that his finest illustrations about the Kingdom and the Christian way of life come from very common tasks. These were the tasks that were a part of his childhood in the carpenter shop; these were the tasks that he knew were a vital part of every life. The work of our hands will say much about the condition of our spirits. Luke reports that even at the dinner itself a dispute arose about greatness. Who will be chairman of the board; who will be bishop in the church that shall grow to continue your teachings; who shall we respect and look up to? "Let the greatest among you become as the youngest, and the leader as one who serves. For which is greater, one who sits at table, or one who serves?" (Luke 22:26-27). Nowhere do we have the name of the one who served the supper and stayed and did the dishes, but I've always had a feeling that as Jesus said this to his disciples he was pointing or at least looking at the one or ones who had cleaned the room and set the table, prepared the meal, and later did the dishes.

I look back over my own life and recall the times when I have felt nearest to God; times when I have felt that perhaps I was "not far from the Kingdom." These times have certainly not been when I was guest speaker and received a flowery and complimentary introduction. They have come when I have been doing my routine and sometimes rather menial tasks. I think back across the years to the individuals who have meant most to me in my ministry. There were professors of note in seminary and there have been Bishops whom I respected and learned from. But somehow my mind keeps going to a woman who always made the coffee and helped prepare and clean up at our church suppers. I remember the day she said quietly to me, "I make coffee to the glory of God." I remember the church I served as a student pastor. It was a lovely little brown church in a grove of oak trees. It was desperately needing paint and had suffered some neglect. A young man about my age was planning to be married in the church. He said to me, "Let's paint it before the wedding," and together we painted the church. We shared some long, hot hours of undistinguished labor, but the church looked splendid on his wedding day and now, thirty-five years later, he and his wife and my wife and I still exchange letters and keep in touch between Wisconsin and Idaho. His paint brush and his willing arm certainly meant much in the life of a young preacher. Who is greatest in the Kingdom? I remember an usher who has already stepped across that thin line that we call death and who has already heard the words "Well done, good and faithful servant." While I was pastor of the church he served I never had to give a thought to details that have been a concern to me in some other churches. Burr loved his church and I knew that the heat would always be turned up and the lights on for services, and more important, things would be taken care of after services. The decoration committee is always more fun than the clean-up committee, but Burr was equally dependable before and after any church event.

Who Did the Dishes?

A wonderful couple, Aquila and Priscilla, are mentioned four times in our New Testament. So many times the great apostle Paul found peace and rest, food and warmth, in their home. I wonder if we would have had his writings if it had not been for their loving care? It is something to think about. We will never know the full importance of their ministry, but I am sure it ranks very high in the eyes of one who said: Who is greatest, one who sits at table or one who serves? One could go on and on listing the wonderful Christians who have served their God by doing the common tasks necessary if life is to proceed and the true meaning of our faith be understood. There are those who feed the hungry, clothe the naked, visit the sick. There are those who cook the food, set the table, and sweep the floors. And always when I come to the Communion service, thinking of the Last Supper of our Lord, the burdens he bore and the grief he felt, what it meant to him to have a place prepared, a meal cooked, and the freedom to sing a hymn and go out into the garden to pray, I wonder: Who did the dishes?

Don't Let It Spoil Your Supper

One night a number of years ago I was riding with a good friend of mine who was a commercial outfitter and guide. It was late summer, the weather was warm. We were riding in some country where we had not been before looking for good places to put hunting camps later in the fall and checking on the number of elk using the country. We had had a long day on the trail and were looking for a place to camp, but since we were in strange country we didn't know any really good places. Darkness was coming on, our horses were tired, and we were hungry. It seemed the trail went on and on with no likely camp spots. Finally we came to a little meadow of sorts, certainly not an ideal camp spot. But there was a pool of water, more a puddle than a pool, and there was some grass for the horses. "Looks like the best we can do," my friend said, and we began to make camp. The water, though a bit stale, was a drink for our horses and we knew that by boiling it we could make it safe to drink and by putting enough coffee in it we could make it fairly palatable.

It was full dark when we had the horses turned out, camp set up, and a good supper cooked. We were just getting ready to eat when there was a shift in the wind and it became obvious that, not too far from our camp, something was very dead.

The smell was not pleasant, probably a dead elk or deer, but one could always hope the wind would shift again. "A pretty rotten place to eat supper," I grumbled.

"You're right," answered my friend, a seasoned mountain man. "And you've got two choices. Eat your supper in this rotten place or go to bed without supper and have a long hungry night. For my part, we've had a long day, I'm hungry, this is good food, and if I were you I wouldn't let something like a bad smell spoil my supper."

Well, I was pretty hungry too, and it was good food, so I did eat my supper. Since then I have often pondered the wisdom of my friend who knew how to take the good with the bad, make the best of all situations on the trail, and live a pretty happy life.

A hungry man, with some good food to eat, in some unpleasant circumstances is a rather good picture of the world in which we live. The more I see of life the more I am convinced that one of the great truths of the Christian faith is that, although we live in a world that is far from perfect, we can learn to live among the evils of the world with such a spirit of hope and purpose that it will not spoil our supper. We will not let the unpleasant, the ugly, the evil, keep us from living the abundant life.

My friend gave me two choices. There is another choice many people take: Go ahead and eat but constantly complain and grumble about the conditions. In this way they manage not only to spoil their own supper, and probably get indigestion, but also to make things miserable for those around them.

The Christian faith is a very practical faith. It helps us to see what is good and beautiful and teaches us to praise God for it. It also teaches us to try to make things better if and when we can. But it faces the fact that there is much that is evil, unpleasant, and nasty in this world, which, with our limited abilities, we cannot change. It is already too dark to move camp; there is no way to locate and eliminate the source of the unpleasant odor. But there is food before us; we can go ahead and eat and not let the conditions spoil our supper.

As Christians we have a challenge to make this a good world, but we have an even greater challenge: to live a good life in a bad world; to partake of the table that is set in the presence of our enemies. It is my conviction that we are living in a time of too much fear and not enough faith. One does not need to be a very keen student to recognize that there is terrible suffering in the world. War is always a present threat; there is famine, disease, overcrowding, and the kinds of energy we have depended on for the past hundred years seem to be declining. But one also does not need to be a very keen student to realize that if you wait until all the problems are solved before enjoying your supper, you will have a long and hungry night. Certainly the worst of the world's problems will not be solved in my lifetime—they may even get worse rather than better. But I can't stop the world and get off, and I have been promised an abundant life. I like to do a bit of free translating of one of the great sayings of our Lord: In the world you will have trouble, but don't let it get you down, go ahead and eat your supper, I have overcome the world (John 16:33).

We hear a lot these days about energy and nonrenewable resources. It may be that for people without faith, this is a crisis, but for the Christian it is a problem, not a crisis, and there is a very important difference. It means we work on it, but do not get emotionally upset to the point that it interferes with our ability to live and love, enjoy and praise, and make the most of what we do have. When it comes to nonrenewable resources, time is the one that is most vital for me. I am fifty-seven and I don't know any way to turn back the clock. I'm not as strong as I used to be, I can't ride as well as I used to, and I know that I'm in the fourth quarter of the ball game. There's not a thing I can do about it, but I'm not going to let it spoil my supper.

I hear disillusioned people saying the church has failed, or the schools have failed, or democracy has failed, because we have not made a better world. And I always wonder: Better than what? This is the only world we have. It is the one God created and the one he gave us for our home. There is unexplainable evil but there is also an abundance of undeserved good. One can concentrate on the evil—one can make oneself sick thinking about it. But I have an idea that the wisdom of my hardworking, practical friend on that dark and smelly night is pretty good advice.

If I want my advice from a more famous source I like to turn to the words of a man named Paul who probably suffered more abuse, saw more heartbreak, injustice, and brutality, and smelled more bad smells than most of us are ever going to experience. He put it this way: "Who shall separate us from the love of Christ? Shall tribulation, or distress, or persecution, or famine, or nakedness, or peril, or the sword?" (Rom. 8:35). He had seen it all: the blood and pain of the arena, the injustice and brutality of the slave markets, the persecution of believers. Of course, if he could have performed a miracle, made it all nice and sweet, he would have done it. But he knew the world isn't like that. It can have a very nasty odor at times. But he also could say: "In all these things we are more than conquerors through him who loved us" (Rom. 8:37). There are times when it certainly is not a very nice world. But don't let it spoil your supper.

Put Your Face in It

As a hounded, thirsty deer longs for a flowing stream, so my soul thirsts for the living God.

—Psalm 42:1 (author's paraphrase)

A number of years ago I was one of the leaders at a Junior High summer camp at our beautiful Camp Sawtooth, a church-owned camp in the Sawtooth Range of mountains in south central Idaho, a magnificent setting. The upper portion of the south fork of the Boise River that flows right through the camp is a crystal clear stream in which one can clearly see a fish or a pebble on the river bottom, even in pools five or six feet deep. The campground is a part of a narrow valley, high mountains rising right at the edge of the camp on either side. The mountains rise in a series of ridges and minor peaks for many miles, so that a hiker can begin at camp and hike in the mountains as far as he wishes—a hike of an hour, a day, or a week. On a minor peak, not too far from camp, a cross has been set up, and the hike to this cross has become one of the popular hikes. It is probably about half a mile in a direct line from the camp to the cross, but it is a steep climb and one can spend several hours climbing at an easy pace. It is possible to climb almost directly up to the cross, but that route is an extremely steep one up a southern exposure which is almost treeless, without water, and it can be a hot, dry climb on a sunny, summer afternoon. I have always preferred going by a route around to the north slope of the hill that takes a more gradual ascent and goes through an area with much more vegetation as well as a number of springs and little streams. The water from the springs is clean, pure, and cold, a wonderful source of refreshment on a hot day.

I was making the climb to the cross one very hot afternoon with a pleasant group of Junior High young people. We had been walking and climbing for an hour or more and were quite thirsty when we came to a spring with a nice flow of water forming a little stream on the hillside. I suggested that we stop for a rest and a cool drink. A little girl who had never been out in the hills before was obviously ready to rest and was quite thirsty. She looked at the water; she looked at me. Then she said: "How can I get a drink? I don't have a cup."

Having spent a great deal of time in the mountains where people are few and water is clean, I had never thought of this problem before and I simply said to her, "Lie down on your tummy and put your face in it." I will never forget the picture of pure joy and satisfaction when she rose up, a big smile on her face, water dripping off her sunburned nose, and said, "Ummmmm, that was good!" Well, it was good. And it filled her very deep and very simple need as nothing else could. It made one wish that all our needs—the hungers and thirsts of life—could be so simply and so adequately filled.

When I returned from the hike I wrote some observations in my "wisdom book." I realized that had we been going directly up the short route on the south slope we would have been terribly thirsty and there would have been no cooling stream for our refreshment. In my journal I wrote: There is no shortcut to the Cross. How true this is. The cross is a symbol of our faith; it stands for dedication and for all that is deeply rewarding and fulfilling in our Christian life. It also stands for struggle and suffering. In attaining it we need to take the long way around. We need to take time to think things out, to learn to work with others, to think before we speak, to have time for resting and growing in our faith, and it is only as we take the long way around that we can make the climb and find the refreshment we need along the way. Very often the discouraged or disillusioned Christian is the one who has tried to run straight up on the steep and streamless side of the hill—trying to reach the Cross by the shortest route. Then he has found steep places, much sacrifice, burning sunlight, but has not found the cooling streams by which to restore his soul before continuing the upward struggle.

The other item I noted in my book, and this may be more important than the first, was this: We often make things too complicated. The thirsty little girl, standing in the presence of sweet, clean, cold water but not knowing how to get a drink, reminded me of many good people today who are searching for a faith, yearning for the living God, when God's love and a refreshing faith is right there with them and really all they need to do is "put their face in it." The faith that can refresh and sustain us as we struggle upward on the paths of life is just as simple as Jesus said it is: "Come to me, all who labor and are heavy laden, and I will give you rest" (Matt. 11:28). We are so used to doing things our own way, drinking only from our own cup, that we fail to recognize the "water of life" unless it is served in a container of our making.

As a pastor and preacher I certainly do not want to make light of the desire to study and the importance of education. I like to read the great theologians and philosophers. But I like to remember that my favorite preacher, the apostle Paul, who certainly had our modern equivalent of a Ph.D., knew full well that when the heat of the day is upon us, and the weary feet refuse to climb because of the burdens and the struggles of life, we are not saved by learning and we are not refreshed from a cup of our own righteousness. In simple faith we come to the gift of God in Christ Jesus our Lord and "put our face in it." Paul would say you do not need the cup of the Jewish law, though he possessed it and loved it. He would not require the cup of Greek philosophy and wisdom, though he admired it. This brilliant, educated, saintly man knew what we all need to know—that the real thirst of the human soul is quenched by springs of living water that are ours for the drinking and in our times of deepest need we must simply put our face in it and be refreshed, renewed, and ready to continue on the upward journey.

This human tendency to make things too complicated is a problem in our relationships with those we love. I have talked with husbands and wives or parents and children or brothers and sisters who need and love each other but who have become separated because of a misunderstanding or an indiscretion that is hard to forgive. They truly thirst for each other but do not know how to "get through" to one another because of feelings of guilt, or ideas of convention, or fear of being rejected. Like the little girl, they stand in the presence of cool water and hesitate for want of a cup. There is a time when you must simply "put your face in it," when you must go to a loved one, put your arms around him or her, and say, "I need you," or, like the prodigal son, simply say I will arise and go—cup or no cup. It is amazing what wonders can take place. How good it can be to put your face in it and find yourself refreshed and with tears of joy dripping from your face saying, "Ummmm, that was good!" How artificial we can be, how we can hunger and thirst for love, in the very presence of it, because we think we must receive the drink in some cup of convention, or must wait until some proper place or more convenient time.

One of the great gifts of scripture is the constant reminder that we need the simplicity of little children and the simplicity of the uncomplicated creatures like the animals and birds that are so often used as illustrations. When I find myself pushed and weary, when I really feel hounded and taunted to the point of my soul's being "cast down within me," I like to turn again to Psalm 42 in which the writer compares his situation to the hunted deer who has been chased by the hounds and is panting for air and desperately thirsty. The deer in his natural wisdom knows exactly what he longs for—a cooling stream. When he comes to it there will be no searching for a cup, no theologizing, no wondering if he is doing it rightly or wrongly. He will simply plunge his face into that cooling stream and know that his deepest need has been filled and he is ready to continue in his struggle to outrun his pursuers, to overcome his adversities, and to find his way to higher, safer pastures.

I would like to revise Matthew 5:3 to read: Blessed are the uncomplicated for they shall find joy and satisfaction. I have spent many days in the mountains in situations in which I would have died of thirst if I had insisted on knowing the source of a stream before drinking from it. No child would ever survive if he had to understand the process of digestion before being blessed by it, or understand a parent's love before being protected by it. A drowning child certainly does not need to know the nationality or even the motives of a lifeguard to be rescued by her, and I cannot wait to understand the mystery of the Cross and a God who could reveal himself in Christ before accepting his love and forgiveness. I want to be well informed, but life is too big, death is too definite, and loneliness is too terrible for me to wait until I have my intellectual questions all answered to accept the love and forgiveness that I need. When my lips are parched and my throat aches with dryness, when I come to the cooling stream I might think for a moment that a cup would be nice, but I'm not going to hesitate to drop right down on my tummy and put my face in it.

Liberation

You were called to freedom, . . . through love be servants of one another.

—Galatians 5:13

The land on which we built our home, and on which we are trying to develop and maintain a fairly attractive yard, was allowed to lie unattended for a few years before we bought it, and the entire area grew a very healthy, well-established stand of quack grass. Quack grass is a hardy perennial with a fantastic underground root system. It is almost impossible to kill out completely, because any root left in the ground will put up new shoots at the first opportunity. In fact, for me,

75

quack grass has become nature's best illustration of sin because it is always present; there are always roots that are not completely eradicated, and it will take over any neglected area of the yard almost at once. In our yard, most of the gardening effort is an effort to replace quack grass with more pleasing and valuable plants.

Being sentimental about the area where we used to live in the mountains of central Idaho, an area where aspen, black birch, and chokecherry were native and in abundance, I have tried to introduce these trees to our yard in Boise and I am having fairly good success, though it is obvious the soil is not just right for my aspen trees. But there is a problem even more serious than the nature of the soil. It is the fact that the aspens must compete with the quack grass. For the small trees this is a very real struggle. The aspen, as well as the quack grass, uses a root system to propagate itself, with new shoots coming up from the roots of a nearby tree. The quack grass grows faster than the aspens, and in my efforts to remove the quack grass I have to be very careful not to destroy any new aspen shoots that may be trying to get a start.

We have had a mild winter, and, though the aspens have been dormant, the quack grass has continued to grow to some extent. Today I have been working to try to free a clump of my little aspen trees from a mat of quack grass that has literally bound the trees, and if permitted to grow unchecked will choke the aspens to death. It has been a tough job to try to set the aspens free from the clutches of the quack grass. For the present my aspens are liberated, but I will have to continue to help them in their fight for freedom for some time to come, and while seeking to liberate them I could not help reflecting on a declaration attributed to Thomas Jefferson: Eternal vigilance is the price of freedom. More than this, I could not help but reflect on the nature of freedom itself. Why was I trying to set them free and what does liberation mean for an aspen tree—or for a person?

In studying biblical passages on freedom, I find that freedom and liberty are used very much for the same concept, depending on the translation one is using. King James uses *liberty* in Gal. 5:1 where most other versions use some form of the word *freedom*. In Luke 4:18, Jesus states the goals of his ministry by quoting from Isaiah: "to proclaim release to the captives . . . to set at liberty those who are oppressed." There is hardly a more definite note in the gospel than the fact that the Good News of Christ brings freedom or liberation or release from something that has kept us from being all that we ought to be. "You will know the truth, and the truth will make you free" (John 8:32). It is interesting that when Jesus said this to some Jewish leaders, they were surprised and said they were not in bondage, so how could they be set free. It is obvious that the Christian idea of freedom or liberation is something more than escape from some person or system that has been holding you against your will; it is not liberation *from* something but *for* something.

Why do I liberate my trees? So that they can develop their true character and grow into the beautiful trees their Creator intended them to be. Really, the most important meaning of liberation is involved with what they will do through developing their potential, not what I do by removing some obstacles. It is this positive use of freedom, the freedom to become something beautiful and useful in God's sight, that is the true meaning of liberation, and a meaning that we can often miss by putting too much emphasis on that which has held us captive, or what has at least seemed to be a limiting factor in our lives. It is possible that in our time, when we speak and think a great deal about freedom and liberation, we have not given enough emphasis to the Christian aspect, which is freedom to become rather than simply to escape.

Some years ago there was a popular song about a man who called himself "king of the road." He was a hobo, a drifter—what in my childhood was called a tramp or a bum. But he was free: free of marriage and family responsibility, free from house payments, free from taxes, voting obligations, jury duty, and the daily grind of reporting to work. He was liberated—for nothing. In seeking his life he had lost it, and I am sure no thoughtful person would envy him. He was liberated from life. And one of the common dangers of our time is our tendency to think of liberation as freedom from restrictions that someone else has placed on us, rather than seeing it as the opportunity to be what God wants us to be. We all carry some chains that are a part of our culture, our marriage customs, our economic system, the political structures around us. But by far the heaviest chains we carry are chains of our own making—chains of selfishness, pride, envy—the kind of chains that can be cast off when we become new creatures in Christ and realize that liberation is giving ourselves to a new way of living—losing our life so we can find it, knowing that we are truly free only when we are totally committed.

Many in our time are crying for more freedom when they haven't the least idea of what they would do with it if they had it. The tragedy of the prisoner is that he spends his time thinking only of escape from the prison rather than in preparation and concern for what he will do with his liberty, once it is given to him. It is easy to beat on the bars of our cage and cry out for liberation without the least thought of what we will do or be if the bars are removed.

We have a fine young organist in our church. When I watch his fingers fly over the keyboard, apparently without effort, I envy him. He is liberated to make the organ sing and he has a freedom I do not have, a freedom from clumsy fingers and ignorance of music. But he did not have this liberation the first time he sat at an organ; nor is it something anyone could give him. He is free to make wonderful music because he has been bound by hours of dedicated practice and an eagerness to grow as a fine musician. I like horses and good horsemanship and when I see a girl on a fine horse in full gallop over a meadow, girl and horse seemingly blended together, I think there is no better picture of freedom—"free as the wind," we say. But that liberation was not something given to her. The first time she mounted a horse she was not free to ride like that at all, nor the tenth time. It took the first few hundred hours of dedicated, disciplined riding just to get to the place where she could feel at ease and in control of a really spirited horse. I am seeing the liberation that comes from commitment, the freedom that is the gift of discipline.

Some years ago I was encouraged to take up the game of golf. It looked simple on TV. You just walk up to a ball, take a swing, and the ball goes sailing down the fairway to lie in a fine position to be put up on the green in one more shot. But when I tried it, it didn't work that way. I was not a liberated golfer. And I have come to the realization that I probably will never be, because one who is free to make the shots I have seen on TV must be much more bound to practice and training than I am able or willing to be. The liberation that I would enjoy on the golf course is not anything anyone can give me, and there is only one way I could ever enjoy it—I would have to earn it by devotion to the game.

In my childhood I never saw much money. By materialistic standards we were poor folks. Yet we were free and liberated. We were free to read good books, hear good preaching on Sunday, and above all we were free to laugh and were truly liberated by parents who had a great faith and a great sense of humor.

So today I have been liberating my aspen trees. I have realized I cannot truly liberate them just by removing the quack grass that is restricting them. The real liberation is something they must do themselves by growing into the form and shape that God has given to aspen trees. These trees have told me something. Christian liberation does not mean escape from our circumstances nearly as much as it means fulfillment of our possibilities. It is only when we are bound by our commitment to love, loyalty, faith, and discipline that we are free to achieve and grow and enjoy. Liberation for my aspen trees means that they can grow into lovely white-barked trees with leaves that quake and shimmer in the lightest breeze and turn to bright gold in autumn. Liberation for me means I can grow in the likeness of one who said that if I try to save my life I will lose it, but if I am willing to give it for his sake, I will find it (Matt. 10:39). As I learn to give, he will give to me—good measure, pressed down, and shaken together, and running over (Luke 6:38).

Carrots,
Cow Parsnips,
& Water Hemlock

During most of my adult life I have owned some livestock and have always been interested in the cattle business. Even now, though I am a city preacher, I own a few cows which are on lease to my son-in-law and daughter. These cows along with many others spend part of the summer on the mountain ranges of Sky Range Ranch near Salmon, Idaho. One of the risks of the cattle business is the problem of poison plants. I suppose there is no better illustration of the problem of evil in the world than the fact that the most beautiful ranges where the cattle go to find the grass they need for their nourishment always contain a certain number

81

of plants that can be deadly. Idaho has many of the well-known poison plants, and Sky Range is no exception, though fortunately all the known poison plants do not occur on the same ranges. We do have two kinds of larkspur, close relative to the lovely delphinium that blooms in the flower garden and which can quite easily be eaten in quantities that can be fatal. Black henbane, containing bella donna, a very dangerous drug, grows well on our ranges, but it is not very palatable and is seldom eaten by cattle unless they are very hungry. Even the delightful chokecherry, which I grow in the yard of our home in Boise and enjoy seeing along the creeks on our ranges, has a poison in the leaves that, in quantity, can kill. It takes about one pound of dried leaves to kill a cow; about three ounces can prove fatal for a sheep.

There are cow parsnips, which are not fatal except in large quantities. We did once have a valuable bull named Ferdinand who was too lazy to climb the hills to get grass so he stayed in the creek bottom and did consume an overdose. Perhaps the most deadly poison on the range is water hemlock, very similar to the plant used in the fatal hemlock brew Socrates drank. At the same time, common carrots are of the same family and not only safe but healthful food.

When I operated Sky Range Ranch and used to ride among my cattle encouraging them to stay away from areas of the range with large concentrations of poison plants, I often reflected on the similarity between cattle grazing on a range where there is the possibility of eating larkspur or death camas and the life of a Christian facing a world in which unexplainable evil is a part of life. When I rode among my cattle and came to a poison plant or a patch of them, I generally took the time to get off my horse and pull up all the plants I could. Sometimes we sprayed certain areas with herbicides. But I knew that, try as I might, I would never eliminate all the bad plants. If I stayed in the cattle business there would always be the risk of an occasional loss of an animal that foolishly ate the poison, even when good grass was available. The best way to reduce such losses is to take good care of the range and never allow the good grasses to be in short supply.

There is something challenging about a world where carrots, cow parsnips, and water hemlock are all in the same family of plants. We may reduce their numbers a little, but we cannot remove poisons from the world. This means that as Christians we will live in a world where there is evil, but we will try not to indulge in it; we will live in a world where we have to make choices. We have tasted the fruit of the tree of the knowledge of good and evil and do not live in the garden of Eden, but a good way east of Eden.

When our children were small we tried to keep the black henbane eliminated from our yard, but we knew that it would keep coming back because it grew around us in the hills, and we knew that the only true protection was for them to learn, as early as possible, not to eat it. The problem of evil is a difficult problem for Christians; we have no final answers in this life. Our eldest daughter posed the problem very early in her life when she asked, ''Why did God make rattle-snakes?'' We really do not know the answer; we do know that snakes with deadly fangs and plants with deadly poison are a part of the total creation and are a symbol of the problem of evil. We don't solve the problem by eliminating all the snakes, but we learn how best to avoid them. We taught our children, very early, to wear cowboy boots, with the jeans hanging down on the outside, making a good baffle for the strike of the average small snake on our ranges. We taught our children, when riding range, not to get off a horse without watching where they put their feet, and to take other reasonable precautions.

As part of our Christian moral concern we try to eliminate evil when we can, but we know our best efforts will make only a limited difference. Our primary effort must be to learn to live in the presence of evil and not be overcome by it. This means learning to make choices, developing a standard of moral conduct, developing character and discipline. Perhaps there is no stronger theme in the New Testament than the challenge to the person of faith to live a good life in a bad world. Jesus said, "In the world you have tribulation; but be of good cheer, I have overcome the world" (John 16:33). "Fear not, little flock, for it is your Father's good pleasure to give you the kingdom (Luke 12:32).

The most prominent writer of the New Testament, the apostle Paul, puts a great deal of emphasis on the challenge of dealing with evil in the world. "Put on the whole armor of God," he tells us, because poisoned arrows are flying around (Eph. 6:11). And we can't get our standards from our culture. Paul reminds us that many things are lawful, but not helpful, so we must not be enslaved or, perhaps, addicted, to anything (I Cor. 6:12). In the well-known story of the wheat and the tares (Matt. 13:24 ff. KJV), Jesus is saying human judgment is too limited to uproot evil without also destroying much that is good. Tares were a variety of wild grass similar in appearance to wheat and possibly poisonous. We are advised to concentrate on cultivation of the good wheat and leave the elimination of the tares to the judgment of God. We certainly know that historically all our efforts to root up evil have not contributed to the creation of what is good, and have often led to fanaticism which has created more evil in its wake. The ultimate challenge for the Christian is not making a world that is a safe place in which to live, but learning how to live, and helping others live, by faith, moral judgment, and Christian discipline—a good, abundant, and joyful life in a world that is actually pretty dangerous and constantly presents to us choices between good and evil.

Cows and sheep, when presented with poison weeds, will sometimes eat them. Our human problem is that we are too much inclined to behave like cows and sheep. The Good News of the Gospel is that God has given us something he did not give to cows and sheep—the ability to make moral judgments, to have standards based on our Christian faith, the ability to say no. This ability to make choices between good and evil is so basic to our human situation that it appears in the very first story in the Bible. Man was created and lived in a garden and was told very plainly that he could eat freely of all the trees but one and of that one he should not eat. If he did, he would be in trouble. He did eat it, and he did get into big trouble (Gen. 2:15-17).

This is the story of our life. We are in a world with much good in it, and much evil. We have knowledge and faith to guide us, and the Spirit of God himself. In a world where evil grows along with the good, we thank God that he has given us wisdom to discern the difference between water hemlock, cow parsnips, and carrots, and the moral character to choose which we will eat.

Prospectors

Most of the commercial activity and settlement in Idaho which led to the organization of the government and the recognition of Idaho as the forty-third state in the Union was the direct result of the gold rush that began in Idaho in 1860. The majority of the older towns and cities started in connection with mining activity, and many of the oldest towns are now ghost towns. Gold fever is a part of our Idaho heritage, and, though much of the gold mining came to an end with the Second World War, after a considerable revival during the Depression of the thirties, the image of the prospector is still very clear in the minds of Idahoans.

Prospecting for gold or other precious metals is still serious business for some and a very interesting hobby for many.

Having lived in central Idaho where mining traditions are strong I have had the opportunity of knowing many prospectors. When I first began my ministry in Salmon, Idaho, in 1944 I was privileged to know many older men who had been prospectors and miners and for whom the search for gold was a way of life. It has been my observation that the true, honest-to-goodness prospector, though generally poor, is a happy, good-natured, and very optimistic person. The prospector is a good symbol of the Christian way of life. He is a living example of a confidence and faith in things hoped for and not yet seen. He is a happy man because he is confident that somewhere there is the mother lode; somewhere there is the bonanza; he lives each day joyfully because he always looks ahead and never backward. Also characteristic of a prospector is his habit of always looking twice. Whenever he picks up a rock, it is with an eye to seeing something good in it.

It is a great thing to go through life always expecting to find something wonderful. This kind of positive attitude adds a dimension to living that makes a person a joy to associate with and adds a note of pleasure to any situation. And it is amazing how often, when we look for something wonderful, we find it.

Christian optimism is not an empty, pollyanna emotion. It is based on a profound faith that this is my Father's world, and my Father's intentions toward me are good. There is a joy in knowing you are in friendly territory and the one who is in control has plans that work together for good to those who love him.

A friend of mine once took me to a fine fishing stream in Montana. As we walked across the fields toward the stream I realized we were on private property, a large cattle ranch, and I had the uneasy feeling that in order to get to the stream, we might very well be trespassing. I asked my friend about it. How reassuring it was when he said the owner of the ranch was a good friend of his and that he had the owner's permission and invitation for us to be on the ranch to enjoy the fine fishing it afforded. Any Christian, knowing a personal relationship with the God who holds the world in his hands, can know a kind of joy in the realization that the place where he walks and works and plays belongs to one who loves him. He is never trespassing.

A prospector's confidence that he will find something good is similar to the assurance that is a part of being a Christian. It is the quality the New Testament calls hope, and Paul lists it as one of the big three along with faith and love: "So faith, hope, love abide, these three" (I Cor. 13:13). The saddest words in life are: "It is hopeless," whether we are speaking of a business enterprise, a troubled marriage, or a confused emotional life.

Hope has great healing powers and can give us strength we did not know we had. I recently had the pleasure of meeting a man who had been a prisoner of war in Vietnam. (John Dramesi has written his experiences in a book called *Code of Honor* [1975].) He escaped twice, was recaptured twice, and suffered a great deal of torture. His survival is something of a marvel. He was asked why he survived. Naturally, he does not feel that he can say exactly why he made escapes, suffered torture, and survived when others didn't, but he says that he credits his survival to four things: purpose, ambition, discipline, and physical fitness. The first two fit closely the description of what I call hope. His life was built around an intense purpose—to survive and continue to serve. He had an overpowering sense of ambition to achieve that goal. This is what hope is all about—the confidence that we can make it, the assurance that we will find it. It is the quality that any true prospector has. He knows there is gold in "them thar hills," and he will not give up until he finds it.

The Christian knows that God's mercy is from everlasting to everlasting, and he will continue to press on no matter how hard the going may be, because "we are God's children now; it does not yet appear what we shall be, but we know that when he appears we shall be like him, for we shall see him as he is" (I John 3:2).

The second quality of the prospector, typical of a Christian and one that serves us well in living a good life, is the habit of never throwing anything away without taking a second look at it. A tourist or hiker may pick up a rock, look at it once, and discard it. But the prospector picks up a rock, looks at it, then looks at it again, holding it at different angles and making sure that he is seeing it in the best possible light, so that if there is some value in it, he will be sure to find it. What a lesson for us all in our relationship to other people. Never judge on first acquaintance, and never write off another person until you have looked at him from every possible angle and made sure to look at him in the best possible light to bring out any color or value that may be within him, even if it is hidden to the casual observer. Surely this is what God does when he looks at us, and he always finds something good because in the light of his love our values appear. He never idly casts us away. He gives the advantage of a second look, and in that second look he finds gold.

Rock hounds are something like prospectors. Instead of looking for gold or silver, they are searching for gem stones. The agates they are looking for have a quality similar to glass—light will shine through them. But on the outside, where the agate is weathered and rough, it looks, in ordinary light, like an ordinary rock. I have observed rock hounds, looking for agates, walking along the banks of Yellowstone River at sunrise or sunset time so that the angle of the sun's rays will shine almost directly through the rocks. In this special light, one can distinguish between the opaque common rocks and the agate, whose beautiful, translucent interior is obscured by a rough exterior. How important it is, whether looking at people or rocks, to take the little extra time and effort required to see them in the best possible light—the light that will bring out their quality and beauty.

The Christian goes through life as a prospector—always with hope, knowing there is something good to be found, something wonderful that is waiting to be discovered. He shares with the prospector a patience that never discards anything—a rock, a friendship, an acquaintance, or even a bitter experience, without having a second look in a better light to be sure that he has seen the best that is in it and has not thoughtlessly thrown away an unpolished nugget of gold or a badly weathered but very precious gem stone.

Today We Picked the Apricots

For everything there is a season, and a time for every matter under heaven.

—Ecclesiastes 3:1

A few years ago I started some fruit trees beside our house, and this year for the first time our apricot tree bore fruit. It blossomed last year, but a late frost took the blossoms. This year it had some lovely fruit. Because I had not made adequate provision for protecting the fruit from birds and bugs, we decided to pick them all a day or two before they were quite ripe, before the bugs and birds got more than their share. The fruit was delicious, and it is a good feeling, after waiting three years, to know that the tree is a good one and that we can look forward to apricots for many years to come.

Each night at bedtime my wife writes in her diary. She is a recorder of events and a writer of chronicles, which I am not. That evening, as she wrote in her little book I asked what she was writing. She replied with great earnestness, "I am noting the fact that today we picked the apricots." Well, I thought, what is so great about the day on which we picked the apricots that one should record it for posterity? Undoubtedly, about this same time next year we will pick them again, and with good fortune, we will be doing it every summer at about this time. I made a comment to this effect and she simply went on writing and pointed out that it will be good to see if they do get ripe at the same time next summer and to know when to expect them to be ready. Of course, one does not argue with this sort of wisdom, though I continued to mull it over for a while. The more I thought about it the more I realized she was exactly right. The day on which you pick the apricots is a great day and worthy of recording in the book of life. The fact that it will happen with a certain degree of regularity does not detract from its importance, but rather adds to the wonder of the event.

One of the greatest causes of discontent and boredom in life is the tendency we have of believing that if something happens with regularity, it ceases to be wonderful, when quite the opposite is true. When spring comes, I can check with Betty's diary and see if the season is a bit late, but wouldn't it be terrible if it didn't come at all? Because it is so dependable, I sometimes forget to thank and praise God for the wonder of it. One of these days I presume Betty will note in her little book that the new grass, when it came in the meadows this year, was green. And so it was. But that is worth noting. What if it were black or white?

It really is a wonderful thing that the grass turned out to be green again this year. It reminds us of the wonder of a God who could have made the world in black and white, but because he loves beauty and chooses to make things wonderful, he has made the world in technicolor. Our ripe tomatoes will continue to be red; yellow apples will be yellow; the autumn leaves will be all sorts of colors.

God could have made drab gray peach blossoms, but he didn't. It may be childish, but I like to think of God going around making things fantastically beautiful just for the sheer fun of it. He could have made the surface of the earth like the surface of the moon, but he didn't, and I'm glad. He could have made everything one long, sunshiny day, but he didn't. Instead he gave us summer and winter, spring and fall. He gave us childhood and old age; he gave us morning and evening; and he looked upon all that he made and he saw that it was good.

There is something fascinating about the migration of birds with the changing of seasons. Here is a large flock of geese. They are contentedly feeding on the wild rice along the edge of the lake in the winter feeding ground. And then, all at once one morning, by some divine alarm clock, they just rise up and start flying north. How do they know when it is time to go? It is about the same time each year, but it is a marvelous thing. We will do well to listen with Job and be humbled: "Where were you when I laid the foundations of the earth? . . . Who determined it's measurements— . . . who laid its cornerstone, when the morning stars sang together, . . . who shut in the sea with doors . . . Have you commanded the morning . . . Where is the way to the dwelling of light, and where is the place of darkness . . . Can you bind the chains of Pleiades, or loose the cords of Orion?" (Job 38).

It is a terrible thing when we mistake the regularity

of life for dullness and believe a thing lacks wonder because it is dependable. The sun came up again this morning, much as it did yesterday. But what a symbol of God's love! And how terrible if it had not come up—or even if it had been two hours late. A child is born—what a common event. Yet how bleak is the life that has ceased to wonder at the miracle of birth. A person dies, another very common event—very common in the sense that it is an event that will be a part of the life of everyone soon or late. This common, dependable event—the closing of a life on this earth—has in it the wonder of God's creation and more than any other event has caused men's minds to turn to God to seek for deeper meanings and more lasting goals than the ordinary material interests that come to an end.

It is the sameness, the regularity, the commonness, of the seasons of life that give them their glory and their meaning. It is good to know that Christmas will come again, at the same old time, that we will sing the same old songs, that there will be joy, and we will mark it on the calendar and note it in the diary. There will be Easter, when the Passover moon is full, and not before. There will be birthdays; there will be weddings; there will be anniversaries when we will hold hands quietly and each know without saying that it is "our song" that is being played. Some read Ecclesiastes 2:24 and say it is pessimistic: "There is nothing better for a man than that he should eat and drink, and find enjoyment in his toil." But really, what is better? I come in tonight, after my day off which I have spent building a fence to keep the stray dogs out of the garden. My wife says, "It is a good fence," and those are good words. It really is a pretty good fence, considering it was built by a preacher. She will write in her book: Today Don finished the fence in the front of the yard. This is not pessimistic—it is profoundly optimistic. A feeling of a job well done is the very stuff good life is made of. The seasons come and go with a wonderful sameness. More and more we come to realize that it is the sameness that tells us that all is in God's hands and we can trust him. Blessed is the person who sees this, accepts it, revels in it with a sense of joy and wonder, knowing that the same God who gives us a sunset will give us a sunrise.

For many years I spent time carefully selecting a Mother's Day card. Then, not long ago, as I began almost automatically looking at the racks to see if the Mother's Day cards were in, I realized that this year I wouldn't need one. Mother had gone and left no forwarding address; she had gone where there is no need of one. It was a strange feeling—but stranger still when I suddenly realized that now I am the older generation. But what an exciting challenge: to try to be the right sort of grandfather; to share with my children and grandchildren the things they will never find in the secular history books; to help them understand the meaning and learn to say, "Lord, thou hast been our dwelling place in all generations" (Ps. 90:1). It is the routine that is wonderful; it is the dependable that is exciting. It is the regularity of changing days and changing seasons that gives real security. I am glad my wife keeps her little book and glad she puts down: Today we picked the apricots.

Jump for
A High Branch

In working my way through college I held a number
of odd jobs. By my sophomore year I had apprenticed
myself to a tree surgeon and found my most interesting
and rewarding work in the pruning and repairing of
trees. I spent my winters in Salem, Oregon, at
Willamette University, finding part-time work there.
The summer of 1939 was spent in Rochester, Min-
nesota, where there are a great many lovely old trees.
In the 1930s Americans in general had not become so
aware of the value of a great old tree as we are now; nor
were we as aware of what can be done to save a tree
that has been damaged by wind or neglected in terms of

regular pruning. What is now a very large and important business—the proper care of trees, particularly large old ornamental trees—was beginning, and I did well in the work, learned a great deal, and thoroughly enjoyed it. Because I was quite athletic and enjoyed climbing I always took the assignments that were high above the street in the very tops of great old maples, black walnuts, elms, or oaks. I have spent many pleasant days of work eighty or a hundred feet above the street or sidewalk. Working, often alone, high up in an old tree was a wonderful opportunity to do a good deal of thinking and to observe a number of things one often misses at street-level—the nesting habits of certain birds, the various kinds of tree toads, (animals that have about the largest voice for their size of any of God's creatures). And in all the areas where I worked, I shared the basic home territory of the squirrel—the delightful little "oak-cat" as the Germans call him, who can travel on the ground but has made a perfect adaptation to life in the treetops. Taking a rest break on some high, shady branch of a giant elm or walnut, I have spent many pleasant moments watching squirrels—watching them fight, court, tend their babies, quarrel over choice nesting places, and above all accomplish athletic feats that would make the finest trapeze artists green with envy.

Being interested in getting through the trees myself with the aid of my climbing rope, and always considering the matter of safety while climbing, I enjoyed watching and learning from these experts in tree travel. They do some fantastic maneuvers, but as they jump from branch to branch, they always jump for the highest one, never, unless absolutely necessary, jumping for the lowest branch on a tree. I am sure there is a reason for this. Though they seldom make a mistake in judgment, and almost always make a good landing on their intended branch, they do occasionally miss, and I am sure they have learned through hard experience, or by an instinct that is the result of survival of those who jumped for high branches, that if you jump for a high branch and miss, there will be another branch you can catch on the way down, but if you jump for a low branch and miss, there is nothing else to break a fall between you and the ground. A hard or even fatal fall may result from your failure to aim high.

As we face the challenges and hazards of life there is something we can all learn from the wisdom of the squirrels. Never set as a goal your lowest possibility. Always aim high—there is no second chance under the lowest branch.

There is a fascinating story in I Kings 17. A man of great faith named Elijah is looking for a place to stay and something to eat. There is a great famine in the land as the result of a drought. Elijah comes to the home of a poor widow who has a flour barrel that is just about empty and a jar of oil that is down to the last few drops. Elijah finds her out gathering some sticks to make a baking fire and asks her for a drink of water. While she is getting the water he also asks her for a morsel of bread. She says she cannot give him bread because even now she is preparing to take the last of her flour and the last of her oil and make a little bread for herself and her son, and then they will die. She has given up. She is making a final jump for the lowest branch on the tree. But the prophet Elijah, with a faith much greater than hers, persuades her to aim a bit higher: "Fear not; go and do as you have said; but first make me a little cake of it and bring it to me, and afterward make for yourself and your son. For thus says the Lord the God of Israel, 'The jar of meal shall not be spent, and the cruse of oil shall not fail, until the day that the Lord sends rain upon the earth'" (I Kings 17:13-14).

We do not know just what miracle happened, but from this incident, we have derived a good expression in our language, "scraping the bottom of the barrel." We know from experience that we have often scraped it and found that there was much more there than we supposed. As we set our goals high and keep looking forward with faith, we find life has for us many more resources than we may dare hope for on the basis of our immediate evidence.

It has been my privilege during the years of my ministry to serve three churches that have all become involved in building programs. In each case we started the program without nearly enough money, but with a great deal of faith and enthusiasm. As we scraped the bottom of the barrel with faith rather than despair, we always found that there was enough to keep the program going and to lead to its ultimate success. In my present church assignment we have just finished building a much-needed church sanctuary, and we started the funding campaign while we were still paying off the debt for an educational building. The wonderful thing about the church board and the building committee I have worked with is that we have had to make a lot of decisions based on faith, rather than money in the bank, and in every case we have followed the wisdom of the squirrels—we have jumped for the highest branch we could possibly hope to make, and, so far, in every case we have made our goal. If some day, with this policy, we miss our goal, there will be a branch or two that we can safely catch on our way down, but heaven help us if we ever set as our goal the lowest branch on the tree. I have decided that in things that really matter we should not ask, Can we afford it, but we should only ask, Is it something God really wants? The goal may seem too high, but we can never lose by trying for it. Jesus tells about a man given five talents who aimed high and took a chance with all five talents, risking everything, and gaining everything. He is compared to a man with one talent who was so lacking in faith that he aimed for the very lowest branch he could see—the branch of security, he thought—and hid his talent for fear of losing it. The man who aimed high made his goal and received the praise of his master, but the man who jumped for the lowest, safest branch, missed even that and lost everything he had (Matt. 25:14 ff.).

Most worthwhile ventures, great or small, involve our acting with a good deal of faith and risk, and it is amazing how often we reach these goals that seemed unreachable. Generally when we settle for the sure thing, the safe bet, the lowest branch in sight, it not only turns out to be dull and uninteresting, because it is unworthy, but it is often more dangerous. We will do well in the adventure of living to remember the wisdom of the simple little squirrel.

The way we use our resources can be a real test of faith. Years ago, traveling in a very dry area, I became extremely thirsty. I came upon an old-fashioned hand-operated pump, the kind that needs to be primed. Beside the pump there was a jug with about a gallon of water in it. A sign above it read: Use this water to prime the pump and be sure to leave the jug full for the next person. I was so thirsty, and it was so far to the next source of water, my immediate reaction was to settle for the stale water in the jug. It was a sure thing. What if I should pour it down the old pump and still not get any water—I would really be in trouble. But the thought of an abundance of cool, clean water from the pump and the confidence expressed by the sign led me to do the right thing, in spite of my thirst. I used the water to prime the pump. As promised, I was able to pump all the fine, cool water I wanted—all I could drink, some to pour over my head to cool me off, and still enough to leave a jug full for the next person. Faith is like this. It doesn't fill all our needs, but it primes the pump that can. It gives us the confidence to jump for a high branch, to find adventure and joy in living and miss the dangerous or dull life that is the sure reward for those who are afraid to take a chance with God.

Through A Clouded Window

For now we see through a glass, darkly; but then face to face.
—I Corinthians 13:12 KJV

Once in awhile, in the area where we live, it rains mud—not a great deal of mud, but enough to make the outside of our windows so streaked and dirty that one cannot get a very clear image of what is on the other side. The mud storm lasts for only a few moments. A wind preceding the rain picks up dust and fills the air with enough dirt that the first drops, coming through the dust-filled air, hit the windows with a splash of dirty water. The rain is so brief that there is not enough clean rain to wash the windows off again, and even if there is, they dry with some definite streaks on them.

Though I am not too good about helping out with housework, I do from time to time help Betty wash the windows. Our system of working together is for me to work on the outside while she is on the inside. It's a good system because, if the light is wrong, there will be a streak of dirt on my side that is difficult for me to see and Betty can point it out. Once in a great while there is a streak on her side that I can point out to her. This is a great time-saver, for if working alone, one would have to run in and out of the house to catch these small streaks.

Washing dirty windows has taught us a great deal about communication. Sometimes the windows have been so dirty that when we first begin to work Betty actually looks funny. The dirt on the window is distorting my view of her. If my only knowledge of her was what I could see, through a very clouded window, I might think her a very odd looking person. But the important thing I have learned is that the dirt distorting my view of her is almost always entirely on my side of the window. As I clean my side, her image improves. Though I can occasionally help her see a speck on her side that she has overlooked, my side of the window is the only one I can do anything about, and if I am to see her for what she really is and what she really means to me, my task is to clean my side of the window.

The great problem we all face in this life is that of understanding—understanding each other and being understood; reaching toward understanding God even as he understands us. The great problem of our human condition is that we are alone and we don't like it. We develop within a capsule of self, and then spend our lives trying to the best of our ability to break out of that capsule, though we never make it completely. For most of us the finest moments of life come when we realize we have reached out of our capsule and actually made contact with someone else so that we are not completely alone. We have really understood and been understood by another—a wife or husband, son or daughter, father or mother—and above all we have made a real step forward in our understanding of God. No one was more aware of this need to know and be known than was the apostle Paul, but he also knew that in this life there are barriers. We can know only in part since our communications are limited by our imperfect human nature. So now we see through a glass darkly, a clouded window, a puzzling image in an imperfect mirror, but we do see. There is a promise of more perfect vision, and we can work on our side of the glass to make the image brighter and better.

In the same chapter in which Paul speaks of imperfect knowledge and an imperfect image in the glass, he also says a great deal about growing up. "When I was a child, . . . I thought like a child, . . . when I became a man, I gave up childish ways" (I Cor. 13:11). Certainly one of the causes of our inability to better understand one another and have more meaningful relationship with God is our unwillingness to grow up and think maturely and realistically. We want to cling to our childish ways of demanding that others solve our problems—of insisting that our problems are caused by the dirt on the other person's side of the window. When we find a new, vital relationship with God; when we clean our side of the window that is between us and God and find that his side has been clean all the time, that he is waiting to look at us honestly and fairly, then we can find the strength and maturity to improve our communications with our neighbor—whether spouse or business partner or someone who owes us money. "You shall love the Lord your God with all your heart. . . . You shall love your neighbor as yourself" (Matt. 22:37-39). There is a reason for the first commandment's being first. Clean your side of the clouded window that keeps you from knowing God; then you will find the help you need to start cleaning clouded windows that have given you a distorted image of your loved ones or those of another color, faith, or economic situation. It does not work to try to put the second commandment first. I see this often in my talks with marriage partners who are having problems. They are trying hard, on a purely human level, to love each other. The window between them remains clouded because they have not cleaned the window through which the image of God's love can bless their efforts to love as they ought.

The greatest cause of divorce is seldom mentioned. It is the fact that in a childish way each is waiting for the other to meet his or her needs, to be the first to clean one side of the window, to make the first step in the direction of forgiveness and mutual understanding. Cleaning windows has taught us that the first step is to get our own side as clean as possible before trying to help the other find the spots that may have been overlooked or difficult to see on his or her side.

It may be overstated, but it has been said that there are really no marriage problems. There are only personal problems that are sometimes aggravated by marriage. And there are really no religious problems. God always does his part, but we often remain separated from him because we are not willing to do an honest and mature job on our side of the relationship.

In this life we do see God and one another through a clouded window, an imperfect glass. But we do not give up hope. Windows can be cleaned, mirrors can be polished. We can clean the window so that we can see each other clearly enough to grin at each other, make faces and have fun, and remember how funny we looked before we started getting the mud off. We can overlook a few spots left on the other side of the window and look forward with faith and hope to that time when we shall no longer see through a clouded window, but face to face, and "understand fully even as I have been fully understood" (I Cor. 13:12).

Campsites on the River

Recently Betty and I joined three other couples whom we have known in various situations over the past years and several other people, who were to become new friends, to take a five-day float trip down the eighty-mile wilderness section of the Salmon River—the roadless portion of the river given the name "River of No Return." In this eighty-mile stretch the river drops approximately one thousand feet. It was great fun. The white-water rapids, with such names as The Devil's Teeth, Elk Horn, Salmon Falls, and Gun Barrel, give the trip a sense of excitement, and the constantly changing scenery of the towering canyon

107

walls gives one a sense of awe and the feeling that must have inspired the psalmist long ago who sang: "In his hand are the deep places of the earth: the strength of the hills is his also. . . . He made it. . . . O come, let us worship and bow down." (Ps. 95:4-6 KJV). What could be better! Days on the white water of the river and nights around the campfire with good friends, reliving old times, sharing tall tales with new friends who were visiting the river for the first time.

For those floating the river, the campsites are small bars generally at the mouth of a creek, often barely large enough to make a camp, but sometimes an area of a few acres. All these campsites have interesting histories. They have been the camping places or homes of a long series of people—Indians, prospectors, hermits, and, in some instances, a family may have lived awhile on one of these isolated sites. Present names carry an intimation of the past—for instance, Lantz Bar where Frank and Jessie Lantz settled in the early 1920s and lived out their lives. On Painter Bar one finds a grave marker with the simple inscription "John R. Painter, died about 1934. Prospector and miner, seeking his fortune." Perhaps most interesting is the Polly Bemis Bar where Charles Bemis lived with his lovely Chinese wife. Polly was a slave girl, born in China, sold by debt-ridden parents, brought to America, and owned by a Chinese businessman in a mining camp. Charles Bemis, a dedicated gambler, won her in a poker game in the 1870s. Bemis was wounded in a gun fight in 1890 and was nursed back to health by his devoted Polly. To express his gratitude he married her legally in 1894, thus giving her the precious gift of citizenship. It is not clear just when they made their permanent home on the river, on one of the larger bars with about fifteen acres of tillable land, but there on Polly Bar at the mouth of Polly Creek, Bemis lived out his life. After his death in 1922, Polly continued to make it her home, living alone in her neatly kept cabin, surrounded by her fruit trees, vegetable and flower gardens, and becoming something of a legend on the river. She died in 1933. (See *Idaho Chinese Lore* by Sister M. Alfreda Elsensohn [1970].)

Our trip on the river gave us five nights with five different camp sites and five days with five different noon stops. Each place we stopped held sights and experiences of interest—Indian paintings, old cabins, orchards untended for many years yet still bearing fruit. At one camp we had a quick change of menu to include dutch oven fresh apple cobbler. At another there were fresh-picked blackberries in the breakfast pancakes.

We landed at each site with expectation and left it with regret—wishing we could stay much longer. But we had our date with the river that never rests but is always moving on. We enjoyed each stopping place, savoring the history, the scenery, the chance to rest awhile, and though we always left too soon, the leaving was made easier knowing there were still more interesting places to explore down the river.

This delightful trip that came too soon to an end is a miniature of the Christian's whole life. We are travelers, not settlers. Always we are pitching our tent and rolling out our bed, only to fold it and roll it up again next day to move on to new and unknown experiences in our lives. How important it is to learn to enjoy all we can while we can, and still be able to move on when we must without undue regret, with a sense of high adventure for what the future holds.

Very soon after returning from the river, Betty and I celebrated with another and larger group of friends the marriage of our youngest child, our daughter Heidi. Life with Heidi, and our older children, has been a good campsite along the river. There have been much laughter, some tears, a lot of learning, some yearning, and surely a feeling that it would be great if

109

we could have stayed longer and explored more. I walked down the aisle of our church with Heidi, took my seat beside Betty, and as we heard the vows spoken and a soloist sing "Sunrise, Sunset" from *Fiddler on the Roof,* we were not ashamed of the tears that were both joy and sorrow, gratitude and regret. We knew without saying it that we were leaving a campsite on the river of life. We were once more folding our tent. The stretch of the river with all the children married and in their own homes is a new and different adventure. We have spent many interesting years at the campsite with the children growing up, and we leave with the feeling that there is so much more we should have done, would like to have done, but there is no stopping the river. So we pack up our gear, look ahead rather than backward, and plan for the next day's travel, its adventure and opportunity, sharing and romance. We are again "just the two of us," and there is so much more to share now than in the brief time we had before the babies came.

Childhood and teen years are for each of us a campsite on the river. There is so much to do, such good fun. We should enjoy it as fully as possible, be in no hurry to leave—yet leave we must for the birthdays do come. The leaving should be made easier by the expectation of good things ahead. For some of us, college years are a brief stopping place—in the long look at life perhaps only a lunch stop—but they can be good years of growing and exploring and finding new ideas.

That first full-time job, the joy of the first years of marriage, children coming and the challenge of being parents, the first home of your own—there are so many interesting places in life. We arrive with excitement and wonder only to find that we cannot ever stay quite long enough to explore all the possibilities and enjoy all the scenery. This is one of the greatest gifts of a loving God—a life in which there is never quite enough time to get bored, a life that always has more interesting things to do than there is time in which to do them.

We are to put down roots, but not too deeply. We are to pitch our tent well, drive our tent pegs securely to withstand any storms, but with the full knowledge that they will be pulled up in the morning, for it is the journey, not the arriving that gives life its meaning. It is the seeking more than the finding that gives life its zest. I recently heard of a woman who is one hundred and one years old. She is having some heart trouble and was told that she could improve her condition with a pacemaker. Her family considered the matter with her doctor then gave her a choice. She said, "I'm ready to go any time, but there are so many things I still want to do. Let's give the pacemaker a try." They did, and she is still doing many things, but she knows she will never get them all done. Her attitude is wonderful, for she is ready to roll up her tent and move on to the next campsite which is still out of sight, around a bend in the river, perhaps through some unknown rapids, but she will find that leaving the place where she now is will be made easier because she does look forward with expectation and faith to that next stopping place.

What an exciting life God has planned for us: seed time and harvest, summer and winter, morning and evening—"a time to be born and a time to die." Like a traveler on the Great Plains we move always toward an intriguing, distant horizon that constantly recedes as we approach it. We approach each new campsite with anticipation; we enjoy each hour we spend in it, then leave it all too soon, because we must press on sharing by faith the keen insight of one of the world's greatest travelers who could quote with confidence: "No eye has seen nor has any ear heard nor anyone fully understood all the good things that God has prepared for those who love him" (I Cor. 2:9, author's paraphrase).